Prais

e

"*Raise Your Frequency & Manifest Abundance* makes me feel seen and nourished. Sherrie Dillard upends conventional offerings to empaths, supports unlearning self and world perceptions that sabotage our potential, and instead provides a transformative process for living in a higher divine frequency. This book is not only medicine for our individual thriving, but also a path to healing our world in these times."

—TESSA THRAVES, Two Crows Hypnotherapy

"An essential read for every intuitive, empathic, and highly sensitive person. Sherrie includes everything you will need to understand and navigate your way in this world so that your beautiful light can shine the way it is intended."

—CHERIE LASSITER, psychic, medium, singer-songwriter, and author of *Amata's Choice*

Raise Your
Frequency
&Manifest
Abundance

About the Author

Sherrie Dillard (Durham, North Carolina) has been a professional psychic, medium, and therapist for over thirty years and has given over 50,000 readings worldwide. She has taught intuition development at Duke University Continuing Studies and has led workshops and classes on spiritual development and spiritual healing nationally and internationally. Sherrie has been featured on radio and television for her innovative books and her work as a psychic detective, medical intuitive, and medium. Additionally, she holds a master of divinity degree in New Thought pastoral counseling. Visit her at SherrieDillard.com.

Raise Your Frequency & Manifest Abundance

A Guide for Empaths, Intuitives, and Sensitives

Sherrie Dillard

LLEWELLYN
WOODBURY, MINNESOTA

FIRST EDITION
First Printing, 2024

Cover design by Shannon McKuhen

Llewellyn Publications is a registered trademark of Llewellyn Worldwide Ltd.

Library of Congress Cataloging-in-Publication Data (Pending)
ISBN: 978-0-7387-7735-1

Llewellyn Worldwide Ltd. does not participate in, endorse, or have any authority or responsibility concerning private business transactions between our authors and the public.

All mail addressed to the author is forwarded but the publisher cannot, unless specifically instructed by the author, give out an address or phone number.

Any internet references contained in this work are current at publication time, but the publisher cannot guarantee that a specific location will continue to be maintained. Please refer to the publisher's website for links to authors' websites and other sources.

Llewellyn Publications
A Division of Llewellyn Worldwide Ltd.
2143 Wooddale Drive
Woodbury, MN 55125-2989
www.llewellyn.com

Printed in the United States of America

Other Books by Sherrie Dillard

I'm Still With You
(Llewellyn, 2020)

I've Never Met a Dead Person I Didn't Like
(6th Books, 2019)

You Are Psychic
(Llewellyn, 2018)

Sacred Signs & Symbols
(Llewellyn, 2017)

Discover Your Authentic Self
(Llewellyn, 2016)

Llewellyn's Complete Book of Mindful Living (contributor)
(Llewellyn, 2016)

Develop Your Medical Intuition
(Llewellyn, 2015)

You Are a Medium
(Llewellyn, 2013)

The Miracle Workers Handbook
(6th Books, 2012)

Love and Intuition
(Llewellyn, 2010)

Discover Your Psychic Type
(Llewellyn, 2008)

*To the female mystics Mirabai, Catherine of Siena,
Julian of Norwich, Hildegard of Bingen,
Therese of Lisieux, and Rabia Basri*

Contents

Who We Are

Are you an empath, an intuitive, or a highly sensitive person, or do you suspect that you may be attuned to unseen energy influences in ways that are hard to define? Do you relate to others and the world through your heart and soul? If you tend to feel what others are feeling and have empathy and a desire to help those in need, you may be an empath. Perhaps you describe yourself as intuitive. You know things without knowing how you know them and can sense, feel, see, hear, and have insights into things that others are not aware of. Maybe you've had dreams or visions of past, present, and future events. For those who are highly sensitive, the world is amplified. Like a lightning rod, your senses respond to and are influenced by both physical matter and nonphysical energy.

Although you may identify as an empathic, intuitive, or highly sensitive person, you likely have some of the tendencies found in all of these orientations. This includes such things as absorbing the energy of others and your environment and receiving sensations, insights, and information through energetic, nonphysical channels. Straddling the physical and spiritual realms, your sensitivity to energy is as natural as your other five senses.

1

At times, being an empath, intuitive, and sensitive can be confusing. Waves of love may open your heart, and you may experience a comforting feeling of connectedness with the natural world and with a nonphysical presence. Then you suddenly feel another's negativity or sadness or tune into their anxious thoughts. To varying degrees, most of us experience the heavy, tired feeling that comes when we absorb the emotional energy of someone who is perpetually negative, moody, or mean-spirited.

Although empaths and the intuitive and highly sensitive have a tendency to want to be of service and help others, we may become exhausted by giving too much and overwhelmed by our own and others' expectations. This energetic overload often manifests through the physical body as the sudden onset of an upset stomach, headache, or aches and pains. Taking on the energy of others can affect our emotional, physical, spiritual, and mental sense of well-being. To protect ourselves, we may try to diminish our intuitive receptivity and better manage our abilities and sensitivities.

Yet we don't always know how to keep the negative and toxic feelings and thoughts of others at bay. We may try to avoid crowds and busy places and stay away from certain people who seem especially negative. To avoid taking on other people's energy, some of us keep conversations shallow and steer away from hearing about others' difficulties and hardships. The need to protect ourselves can become so great that we may stay home and avoid people altogether. Devising ways and strategies to keep ourselves from absorbing the energy of others and nonphysical influences may seem to be a never-ending process. The constant need to feel safe from absorbing and feeling unwanted energy may keep us on edge and wishing that we were not intuitive and sensitive.

To better understand the challenges that come with feeling, sensing, and taking on the energy of others, we may search for helpful books, take classes, and visit professional intuitives or healers. As we gain more knowledge and awareness, we become better at identifying empathic and intuitive sensations and feelings and deciphering their meaning. However, the path to accepting our gifts and further developing them is seldom straightforward. Assumptions and stereotypes of what it means to be empathic, intuitive, or highly sensitive can create a barrier to fully actualizing our potential. The judgments and opinions of family and friends may cause us to hesitate or inhibit our desire to further explore our essential intuitive nature.

Intuitive, empathic, and highly sensitive individuals are often described by the unique vulnerabilities that make it challenging to live in this world. We are often misunderstood and judged as weak, odd, or even psychologically deficient. In the extreme, we may be perceived as being delusional, spacey, and unintelligent escapists who cannot handle the pressures of everyday life. Our special contributions, strengths, and abilities are often minimized and undervalued. These kinds of assumptions, along with our tendency to feel, sense, and absorb negative, uncomfortable, and confusing energy from others and the environment, may halt or sabotage our efforts at self-understanding and self-acceptance.

The special attributes and traits of intuitive, empathic, and highly sensitive individuals are rarely seen and acknowledged. We are insightful, wise, kind, loving, and natural healers and often have an intimate connection with spiritual presence. While we are known for being caring, sensitive, and compassionate, we have a tendency to be taken advantage of by others. With a pure heart and spirit, we may be attracted to those who are lost, hurt, and needy. Unfortunately, we might also trust the untrustworthy, and in our desire to help others, we may take on too much.

If you are an empath, an intuitive, or a highly sensitive person, you might feel like you don't fit neatly within the parameters of the predominant five senses of material reality. However, it is often from the more logical and rational sources of intelligence and the material viewpoint that we are defined and judged. Empaths and the intuitive and sensitive can feel like a round circle trying to fit into a square peg.

Even though we cannot be fully known and understood through the perspective of the material world, this is where we often look for answers. All too often we try to adjust to worldly and cultural standards and compromise our authenticity and well-being in the process. We can never fully know ourselves or be known and understood by others through this limited and close-minded approach. The awareness of those who are empathic, intuitive, and highly sensitive is expansive, as we feel, see, know, and are aware of more than others. When we try to adjust and dial down our awareness, we lose our most magical and powerful essence. It is only when we allow ourselves to be fully who we are that we become stronger and more empowered. Although we may desire to be known and accepted by others, feeling lonely or odd and different comes from not being true to ourselves.

Don't tiptoe around your fears and sensitivities, apologizing to others and compromising your authenticity. We are not here to carry the burden of others or to absorb stressful, chaotic, or harmful energy. All too often we allow others, our fears, and a lack of knowledge to limit our development. We stop short of fully actualizing the benefits and potential of our innate abilities and gifts. Wherever you are in the development of your empathic and intuitive abilities, there is more to know, feel, experience, and be.

If you have been waiting for someone to acknowledge your power and gifts, know that I see and know the beauty and destiny of your heart and soul. My motivation for writing this book isn't to decry those who would unfairly label and misconstrue what it means to be empathic, intuitive, and highly sensitive. Instead, I hope to awaken your heart, mind, and soul to your transcendent destiny.

About This Book

This book isn't so much concerned with teaching you how to develop your intuitive and psychic skills and abilities in the traditional way that it has been taught. Instead, it will encourage you to unlearn the accepted approach and perceive the full potential of your extrasensory self. In these pages, you will discover empathic and intuitive sensitivity to be the channel through which you can manifest all forms of abundance.

Exploring the potential of empathic, intuitive sensitivities has been my passion for many years. Like many people, I was aware of the unseen realm from a young age. As a teenager, my extrasensory awareness blossomed. At the age of seventeen, I found myself on my own, negotiating my sudden ascent into adult life. The challenges of working two jobs to pay for a small room in someone's attic consumed most of my time and energy. However, this didn't slow down my intuitive and empathic awareness. With no help or encouragement, it continued to flourish. Intuited feelings, visions, insights, sensations, and impressions flowed through me like a raging river. However, I didn't always know the meaning or purpose of what I received. Mostly, I felt alone and lost.

One dark night after my shift washing dishes at a restaurant, I sat outside in a wooded area staring up at the stars. Suddenly a warm flow of energy seemed to break through my closed heart. As this energy flowed through me, my body begin to quiver and shake and I became lightheaded. Despite the strange sensations, I wasn't afraid and instead felt comforted. Through soft whispers, a presence assured me that everything was going to be okay. The accumulated stress that I had been feeling seemed to slide off of me. Feelings of love and peace crept in, and I didn't want whatever I was feeling to go away. As the intensity subsided, I knew that this presence would always be with me. After this experience, the circumstances of my life started to change and improve. I became more aware of this loving and wise presence and listened for the soft whispers of support and assurance. Unexpected positive opportunities came my way and guiding synchronicities unfolded.

Over my thirty-five years as a psychic and medium and teacher, I've become aware that the possibilities and expansive nature of our extrasensory awareness are boundless. Receiving intuitive and empathic messages and guidance can be insightful and helpful, but this is just one aspect of what our innate abilities and sensitivities offer.

Thought-based, analytical reasoning cannot penetrate the realm of nonphysical phenomena. Instead of trying to adapt and fit into the material perspective, we are called to listen more closely to our heart and spirit. We aren't here to live a small life of defensive protection and continually fear the negativity and narcissists of the world. We are much too powerful for this. The root of our tendency to take on unhealthy and negative energy is not in the outer world, but within ourselves. It is our undeveloped and misunderstood relationship with our spirit that leaves us susceptible to absorbing the energy of others and becoming confused and overwhelmed. While we may focus on controlling our exposure to people, situations, and influences that feel harmful, threatening, or toxic, our biggest challenge is to lift our awareness into the higher realms of pure creative energy.

We tend to define empathic and intuitive awareness as the ability to intuit, see, know, feel, and become aware of energy information. However, there is a deeper evolutionary mystery calling out to you. For those of us who are empathic, intuitive, and highly sensitive, the process of ascending to higher states of consciousness and transcending material limitations begins with the awareness that we can choose the energy that we absorb and feel. As we heal old wounds, release repressed emotions, and cut energy cords, our consciousness expands and we access divine creative forces. From this higher-vibration perspective, the possibilities are endless. We no longer attract chaotic and harmful energy from others and the environment and are not bound to the laws of the material world. Instead, the activity of divine presence at work within our consciousness becomes the channel through which we receive enlightened guidance and healing and manifest our highest good. Absorbing the higher frequencies of divine energy can manifest in such tangible forms as an increase in finances, career opportunities, abundance in all things, and harmonious relationships. Through discussion, experiential exercises, and guided meditations, this book takes you through this transformative process step-by-step.

We are messengers for a higher divine frequency. In a world that often seems to be barreling toward catastrophe, fully activated and healed empaths, intuitives, and sensitives are an enlightened influence. With innate compassion, clear insight, and a desire to heal and be of service, energy sensitives are a potent force for planetary awakening and transformation. Instead of avoiding others and withdrawing from the world, we are here to illuminate the darkness and guide others with insight, wisdom, and love. Empaths and the intuitive and sensitive walk a sacred path. Even when we are not aware of it, the pure light is calling us into greater bliss and joy.

PART I

You Belong
to the Light

CHAPTER 1

When the Light within You Begins to Peek Through

There is an invisible force of love leading us to our destiny, a destiny that speaks to our body, mind, heart, and spirit and is beyond our purely human comprehension. A few of the ways that we are guided to our destiny and full potential are through inner intuitive whispers, the urgings of our heart, and synchronicities. Sometimes we pay attention, listen, and understand these silent messages, but not always. When we ignore the small nudges, the impetus to evolve might show up in our life as upheaval or challenges that force us to evaluate our current choices and look within. In noticeable and sometimes more subtle ways, such things as our dreams, desires, or discontent or issues in our finances, relationships, or health attempt to get our attention. The roots of change always arise from within the self, even when change appears to come from outer influences.

For some, the call to evolve might occur through a spiritual emergence that awakens their intuitive and empathic gifts and potential. Through intuitive sensitivity and the expanded awareness of things not normally seen and felt, we discover aspects of ourselves not previously known. How we greet intuitive and empathic sensations, feelings, knowing, and awareness when they surface either supports our growth and evolution or keeps us stagnant when inertia takes over. When we are curious and open to the further exploration of extrasensory experiences, our true authentic self breathes a sigh of relief and inches closer to full expression.

In the midst of the budding desire to further investigate our awareness beyond our five senses, many experience sudden doubt and apprehension. We find ourselves resisting and questioning the unexplained insights, feelings, and other types of phenomena we are experiencing. Instead of opening our heart and mind, we cling to the safety and control of the known and the rational and logical way of perceiving things. Our trust in our ability to navigate the expanding intuitive landscape may be flimsy and offer us no assurance or comfort.

Yet it is only when we recognize our fear and still step into the unknown that our power awakens. While our ego self may recoil from the simplest digression from the norm and our routines, the spirit delights in it. Our physical and biological nature directs us to seek safety in the familiar, even if it is not desirable. It is our spirit that is willing to dive into opportunities and creative activity and explore possibilities. Despite our collective innate trepidation and resistance, more and more people are experiencing increased episodes and experiences of empathic and intuitive sensing, feeling, knowing, and awareness.

Not only is our spirit encouraging us to increase our awareness and acceptance of our extrasensory awareness, but external factors are moving us in this direction as well. One of the unexpected influences that has made it possible to be better informed about what is happening in distant places and communicate with people around the globe is our advancing technology. Our ability to reach out and know and feel what another is experiencing has become less dependent on physicality. We no longer believe that we have to be in someone's physical presence to be emotionally, spiritually, or intellectually connected to them. On any given day we may be exposed to the emotions and thoughts of others in a way that doesn't occur in our face-to-face connections. Increased remote connection and communication has lessened our reliance on physicality. Our ability to know others, feel their feelings, and even experience a level of intimacy with them without being physically present has strengthened.

As our ability to know what others are experiencing in remote and distant places expands and increases, the spark of empathy is ignited. Even though we have no physical or personal relationship to such people, we may feel the injustice they have endured and speak out when we see others being denied basic human rights or suffering from abuse or the ravages of war. On fundraising sites, we may give money and emotional support to those who are sick and in need of treatment and to those facing difficult challenges. In our heart, we hold the virtual hand of those we have never met when they suffer a loss or disappointment. To those who are confused and lonely, we offer help and support. We feel their pain and do what we can to help them even though we may have never met or spoken to them.

Not only do we open our hearts and minds to those in need, but others give to us in return. The challenges and successes of those at a distance may be a source of strength and influence us in positive and empowering ways. While sitting quietly alone in our home or office, perhaps behind our computer or on our phone, our heart opens and we may feel the energy of others. Through remote interactions with others, we are becoming comfortable with relying less and less on being in another's physical presence to feel a genuine connection to them. This is encouraging our development into a more expansive and sophisticated energetic sensitivity.

As we increasingly relate and respond to others' thoughts, emotions, and experiences, our empathy, sensitivity, and intuition emerge to lead us. Just as our five senses have given us the ability to understand and live in the physical world, we are beginning to trust our energetic sensitivity to navigate a new path.

Expanding Awareness of Our Energy Environment

Communication and connection to others and the world through advancing technology is not the only factor influencing our heightened energy sensitivity. In response to increasing levels of stress, insecurity, and anxiety, we are looking to mind-body-spirit practices such as energy healing, yoga, and meditation for healing and relief. In addition to helping us release tension and stress, these practices encourage an expanded awareness of our subtle energy.

For instance, energy healers, massage therapists, and other healing practitioners may help us become aware of blockages and stuck energy in our body. Yoga instructors teach us how to focus inward and tune into the flow of energy through our body for healing and rejuvenation.

Through energy-sensing awareness, we may have the intuitive insight that the tightness in our neck or back is connected to a recent disagreement with a family member or problem at work. As we breathe and practice moving energy through the body, the knots and tightness loosen and the pain dissipates. Soothing sensations move through us as we discover ways to take care of our energy health. As we become empowered to work with energy, we experience increased positive outcomes.

Our ability to sense and feel energy in our body increases our intuitive and empathic energetic receptivity. Surprising intuitive insights, sensing, feeling, knowing, and aha moments are more common. Energy awareness becomes more than an abstract concept. Beyond the confines of physicality, we experience ourselves as energy beings as well. Our mind is calmer and our body relaxes as our subtle energies align and we experience a greater sense of wholeness. In this state of inner awareness, we move beyond the ego and may feel the energy within and surrounding us as expansive and engaging. Our intuitive sensitivity is heightened and we become more comfortable with the intangible and unseen. Energy is no longer empty, inert, and lifeless; it is alive and communicative and speaks to us through such things as sensations, insights, feelings, thoughts, and dreams.

Sometimes our sensitivity to energy is understated and barely detectable. For instance, we might experience a slight buzz or tingling in our head when we are with a particular person, during meditation, or when reading. As our sensitivity to energy as emotion or feeling increases, our empathy, compassion, and desire to be of service to others might also get stronger. An awareness of others' sadness, distress, and suffering opens our heart with a genuine desire to be helpful.

Our energy sensitivity and increased awareness might also be spurred on by upheaval and change in our day-to-day life. Through a challenging or traumatic event or the inner ache of emptiness and loneliness, we might suddenly become aware of the presence of a loved one on the other side. We may feel the soft warmth of love and assurance when we are troubled or receive enlightened insights from nonphysical beings. When material pursuits, outer success, or accepted norms are no longer satisfying, we may feel led to pursue a more spiritual path and begin to pay attention to our dreams and signs and synchronicities.

Perhaps you have always been sensitive to energy. Do you experience feelings, sensations, sudden insights, or synchronicities randomly that are surprising or maybe perplexing? Maybe your stomach tightens or flip-flops or you sense a wave of energy and your mood shifts for no apparent reason. Have you ever seen orbs or flashes of light that no one else seems to notice? Perhaps you have suddenly felt a presence close to you or felt a reassuring hand on your shoulder. Although you may struggle to adequately describe the random intuitive sensations, feelings, and sense of knowing that you experience, they don't feel odd or unusual.

Signs of Energetic Sensitivity

Here are some telltale signs that you are energetically sensitive:

- Random sensations of energy moving through your body, especially up the spine or neck, and tingling in the head
- Seeing flashes or streaks of light or orbs
- The hairs on your arms or the back of your neck stand up or tingle for no apparent reason.
- A sudden sensation of heaviness in your head, arms, shoulders, or legs
- A rush of energy moves through your body, causing your arms, legs, feet, or other body parts to twitch.
- The awareness that a spirit presence is close
- An uncomfortable feeling in your stomach and solar plexus upon meeting new people

- Seeing random colors in the air, such as purple, white, gold, or gray
- Sensing warm or cold spots or waves of energy in your environment
- Seeing inner images or visions of symbols, places, or people you don't know
- The feeling that someone you know or have just met is going through a difficult time
- Becoming aware of the presence of a loved one on the other side or an angel or other spirit being
- Feelings of dread, negativity, or fear for no apparent reason
- The feeling that you are not alone
- Sensitivity to electronic stimuli, wireless internet, microwaves, or other invisible waves of electromagnetic energy
- Unexplained feelings of positivity, elation, or joy
- Buzzing in your head or dizziness
- Feeling another's feelings, even if you don't know the person well
- Waking during the night and feeling a warm and loving presence
- A feeling of *déjà vu*: the feeling of having previously experienced an event that is currently happening
- The awareness that you know another person upon first meeting them
- Sensing a spiritual presence that is sending you insights, information, or helpful guidance
- The awareness of another lifetime—where you lived and events from that life

- A sudden dull or sharp headache when planning a trip or making arrangements to meet someone or go someplace
- Waking at night with the awareness of what another is feeling or experiencing
- Feeling uncomfortable in specific environments or locations for no known reason
- Sensitivity to overhead or bright lights (especially fluorescent lights), noise, crowds, or smells
- Some foods, drugs, medications, and types of alcohol affect you in unusual and adverse ways. Normal dosages and amounts are too potent.
- Random physical sensations that seem to come and go, such as a racing heart, twitching, feeling spacey, prickles in your gut, or unexplained aches and pains

These are just some of the ways that the energy of others and the environment can influence and affect us. Some people experience energy in a more visceral and physical manner, while others are more inclined to feel the emotions of others or see inner visions and images. Here are some of the ways clients and friends of mine have described their experiences.

- "I started thinking about my friend Jill last night, then my stomach started to hurt. It feels like she is going through something difficult. I'm going to give her a call."
- "I was excited about getting together with my old friends. Then an hour into dinner with them, I suddenly had a headache and felt overwhelmed. It felt like waves of energy were coming at me. I have no idea what was going on."

- "I was immersed in this new novel and I looked up and saw a white orb right in front of me. It slowly moved through the room and then dissipated. I think this was my grandfather's spirit. I don't know why. It just felt like he was there with me. Sometimes I see flashes of light, mostly mauve and purple. It feels like my loved ones who have passed over are close. My family thinks I'm crazy."

- "Being around people all day, even those I love and care for, makes me so tired. After listening to their issues and problems, I feel so drained. I want to help them and give more, but I am so depleted. People just suck the life out of me."

These and similar types of experiences are more common than you might think. To varying degrees, we all intuit, absorb, and are sensitive to the energy around us. This happens naturally and without effort. For some, this is more accessible and obvious. Those who notice their random feelings and sensations and are attentive to them are also more likely to receive helpful insights and inner guidance.

Common Characteristics of Empaths, Intuitives, and Highly Sensitive People

The world is in a constant state of evolution. We are wired to create, imagine, dream, generate new ideas, and peer into the unknown. As we move forward into greater awareness of the subtle energy within ourselves and in our environment, our evolution speeds up. Empaths and those who are intuitive and highly sensitive are all energy-sensitive and often experience and develop the following characteristics and other similar ones.

Empathic

Many people who are sensitive to energy are empaths. Empaths intuit and soak in the emotional energy of others and the environment. With a deep capacity to care and have compassion for others, empaths are loving souls who are drawn to those in need. They can intuit, sense, feel, and be affected by what others might not be aware of. Kind, caring, and vulnerable, empaths are able to feel and respond to others' wounds and difficulties with emotional depth and understanding and are natural healers. Unfortunately, they are also prone to being taken advantage of. At higher levels of consciousness, empaths can feel, intuit, and absorb the vibrations of divine healing and love.

Intuitive

Intuition is the ability to know or be aware of energy information and knowledge without knowing how we know it. Sometimes intuitive insights and awareness come to us through our thoughts, feelings, dreams, visions, or a sense of knowing. It is also possible to intuit energy information through inner hearing, smells, sensations, gut feelings, or vibes. To varying degrees, those who are energy-sensitive are intuitive.

Highly Sensitive

People who are highly sensitive tend to absorb intuited energy into their physical body but don't recognize that they are doing this. They assume that their sensitivities are due to outer stimuli, such as crowds, constant activity, chaos, and disorganization. Scents, smells, the feel of certain textures, noise, and bright lights can cause stress, anxiety, overwhelming stimulation, and even physical aches and pains. Acts of kindness, love, and other positive states are calming and nurturing, while violence of any kind, meanness, jealousy, and negative feelings and actions can have deep and lasting adverse effects. Most highly sensitive individuals are also intuitive and empathic.

Spiritual Awareness

People who are energy-sensitive are likely to have an inner awareness that there is something beyond the physical world. However, they may not always know how to define or articulate what this is. This knowing can be so acute that they might assume everyone is able to sense that there is something that exists outside of the physical boundaries. From a young age, many have felt the comforting and loving presence of spirit beings. The feeling of an unseen presence may at times feel personal and intimate. It speaks to their concerns and guides them when they are in need and helps them to feel loved. Spiritually aware individuals are often intuitive and empathic and heart-centered.

Like Being Alone

Many who are energy-sensitive feel that they can breathe deeply and relax only when they are alone, as being in the company of others can be overstimulating and overwhelming. It's not just what others say or do; just feeling and taking in the energy of others can create tension and stress. Many instinctively become guarded and feel a need to protect themselves from others' energy. When alone, those who are energy-sensitive have a better chance to think their own thoughts, feel their feelings, dream their dreams, and just be.

Rich Inner Life

In part, energy-sensitive people enjoy being alone because this affords them the opportunity to listen, feel, and get in touch with their rich inner life. Imaginative, dreamy, creative, and full of ideas, they need the time and space to go within and just be.

Because the lines between imagination and intuition can be blurred, it is not always easy to differentiate between the two. The energy-sensitive may discount intuitive images, sensations, and knowing, believing that whatever they are receiving and experiencing is *just their imagination*. However, imagination and intuition work together to help us interpret the meaning of energy information.

Truth and Justice

Those who are energy-sensitive have an inner sense of truth, fairness, and justice and a sense of what is right. This might not always be in alignment with worldly or popular standards. With an inner aptitude for sensing a higher order, their beliefs may not always align with the accepted norms of what others feel is fair and right. Their sense of truth may stem from life lessons and challenges in past lives as well. They might also have the ability to sense the higher purpose of the challenges and obstacles they encounter.

Sense the Outcome of Actions and Beliefs

For energy-sensitive people, energy is not limited by time and space. Their perception transcends time. Because of this, they may be able to perceive the consequences of actions and choices long before others do. This might feel like simple common sense to them. However, they can see the big picture and predict what others might do long before it happens. Energy sensitivity might extend into the development of precognition, which is the ability to know, see, feel, sense, and predict the future.

Time Can Be an Issue

Do you tend to lose track of time? Maybe you find yourself constantly checking the clock to make sure you are not early or late. Do you feel like you don't have enough time to do everything you want to do?

Those who are energy-sensitive may feel out of sync with time. They may find that they are continually rushing or trying to catch up with earthly time. Some who are out of sync with time know and sense what is going to happen in the near or distant future.

At times, energy-sensitive individuals will conceive of an idea or have an awareness of goals they would like to achieve, yet they have difficulty going through the steps to make this happen. In the spiritual realm, creation is spontaneous and there is no lag between idea and expression. Here in the physical world, we operate within the constraints of time and space, which can be challenging for the energy-sensitive. Energy exists in the present, now, and doesn't adhere to the material laws of time and space. However, in the physical world, we experience time as linear and must be patient and often wait for our ideas to manifest.

Desire to Be of Service

If you are energy-sensitive, you likely enjoy the positive and loving feelings that come with helping, sharing, and giving to those in need. Empaths, intuitives, and sensitive people populate the helping professions. If their profession is not focused on being of service, they give to friends, family, neighbors, coworkers, and members of the close and distant community.

Although these individuals are compelled to be of service, it can be challenging for them. When another is suffering, they may suffer along with them, feeling their pain as if it were their own. The grief and confusion of others may penetrate deep into their heart and soul and motivate them to do all they can to alleviate the other person's suffering.

The energy-sensitive may have a desire to reach out to others and be of service without being prompted or asked. They can feel another's feelings without restraint and are motivated to act from the well of love churning within. However, the willingness of energy-sensitive individuals to give freely of their time and resources is not always reciprocated. When they give to others without restraint, they might later feel that they are not appreciated or valued.

Ability to Heal

Many who are energy-sensitive choose helping professions that involve some form of healing. They are medical professionals, bodyworkers, counselors, religious and spiritual leaders, and New Age practitioners. They are often attracted to different forms of energy healing, as both a giver and a receiver. The higher vibrations of positive and divine energy are especially restorative and beneficial to the mind, body, and spirit of these individuals. Empaths and intuitives are natural conduits of energy and can be the channel through which others experience healing.

May Lose Their Sense of Self

Energy is not limited by physical boundaries. Those who are energy-sensitive might feel a closeness and connection to others no matter how far away they may be. They are often able to feel and sense the feelings and thoughts of those they care for from afar.

Some who are energy-sensitive feel so connected to those they love that they merge with them. They might feel the same feelings, share the same beliefs and perspectives, and even begin to look alike. If an energy-sensitive person forms this kind of energetic union with another or with a group over a long period of time, they may lose touch with their core authentic self. When relationship boundaries become blurred, they may no longer be aware of their own needs and sense of self.

Spurts of Energy Stamina and Depletion

Those who are energy-sensitive may have boundless energy. They are able to accomplish goals and get things done and may not need a lot of sleep. However, this usually isn't long-lasting. After a period of energetic activity, it might all of a sudden become difficult for them to focus and get anything done. It may feel as if everything requires too much effort and is a drain on their system. Their energy levels are influenced not just by their physical activity, but also by the people and happenings in their environment.

The Natural World Reenergizes Them

Energy-sensitive people are often attuned to the cycles of the moon, the changing constellations of the stars and planets, seasonal shifts, and other occurrences of the natural world. The universe is streaming with energy that can affect their personal energy levels.

Being in nature is especially calming and restorative for these individuals. Blue skies, the sun's rays, a starry night, and bodies of water may clear their mind, boost their energy, and provide them with a sense of peace. Absorbing energy from the natural world can be especially healing and essential for their mind-body-spirit wellness.

Sensitive to Negative and Toxic People

It's no surprise that the energy-sensitive have an aversion to those who are disruptive, argumentative, and negative. Depression, exhaustion, anxiety, and stress, as well as physical illness, can result from being in the presence of negative and toxic people for a long or even a brief period of time.

Energy-sensitive individuals are often uncomfortable with conversations that revolve around small talk. They may especially dislike being in the company of those who are critical and judgmental or only desire to impress others. Forming authentic personal connections is essential for the energy-sensitive.

Drawn to Positive Energy

Empaths, intuitives, and sensitives are drawn to charismatic teachers and leaders and others who have an enlightened and positive perspective. They may seek out physical locations that contain energy portals or were inhabited by ancient spiritual communities. Many who are energy-sensitive enjoy being part of groups that practice such things as meditation, chanting, yoga, rituals, and other stimulating spiritual practices. People bonded together by uplifting and heart-centered activity intensifies the good feelings.

Awareness of Spirit Beings

Those who are energy-sensitive are often able to sense and feel when a nonphysical presence is in their midst. This might be a visit from a loved one on the other side, an angel, or a multidimensional or divine being. Some will see or sense nonphysical beings as orbs or streaks of light or color, while others might see them through their mind's inner eye as images and in visions. The energy-sensitive might also sense, feel, or hear messages from otherworldly sources through inner hearing.

Moving Forward

Not only has the advancement and our acceptance and awareness of energy sensitivity and the spirit realm evolved, but so have we. In almost every area of mind-body-spirit practices and intuitive and empathic awareness, there has been rapid expansion and increased understanding. Our sensitivity to energy continually changes and unfolds in unpredictable ways. We may begin to feel and sense the emotions and thoughts of others. Then a short time later we may experience new modalities, such as seeing visions, having foreknowledge of events, and sensing loved ones who have passed over. When we are tired or stressed, we may be more sensitive and easily feel overwhelmed with the energy we absorb and receive from others, while being in nature and with those we love supports our inner sense of harmony and centeredness.

Our sensitivity to energy is fluid, and how we respond and react to it varies depending on such things as our moods, fears, and expectations. Sometimes we might ignore and deny the subtle whispers of our empathic, sensitive, and intuitive nature out of ignorance or apprehension. We may try to do our best to rationalize what we are experiencing as being nonsense or insignificant mind chatter. However, we soon learn that attempting to block or shut down our sensitivity to energy leads to feeling detached, anxious, or distant. Suppressing our inner sensing may also lead to an inner pressure, which eventually emerges and floods us with feelings and sensations. When we feel as if we have no power or control over what we are experiencing, we may even wonder if we have a psychological or emotional issue. Some may seek out a therapist or New Age practitioners to better understand the unusual feelings, sensations, and awareness they are experiencing. Then, for no known reason and despite our previous resistance, our energy sensitivity may suddenly bring us feelings of warmth, love, and comfort and we become more trusting. We begin to welcome unexplained sensations, feelings, awareness, and insights and are ready to further explore our extrasensory awareness. Throughout our journey with intuitive and empathic awareness and high sensitivity, we will want to fully embrace it at times, only to then want to run as far away from it as we can a moment later.

In the past, many believed that it was only special, gifted, and rare individuals who had access to the spiritual and energy realms. More and more, the awareness that we all have some degree of intuitive, empathic awareness and high sensitivity is increasing. While our experiences vary and span a broad spectrum, we are becoming more comfortable feeling, sensing, knowing, and experiencing extrasensory phenomena. Just as all of life continually evolves, the potential and possibilities of what the unseen realm offers are moving us forward into new territory.

Our spiritual challenge is to acknowledge and accept our energy sensitivity. This is the starting point through which we can become increasingly aware of the potential of intuitive and empathic awareness and high sensitivity. Instead of denying our multidimensional nature and trying to control and manage it, we can accept it as a natural outgrowth of our expanding consciousness.

In the next chapter, we explore how the obstacles that we commonly confront with intuitive and empathic sensitivity can be used as signposts to guide us to the manifestation of our greater good. While the emphasis of intuitive and empathic sensing has been on the development of abilities and skills, there is greater gold in our extrasensory awareness.

CHAPTER 2

When the Obstacles Become the Path

Energy sensitivity is a form of intelligence. When we allow our empathic, intuitive, and highly sensitive nature the space to expand and reveal itself, insights, synchronicities, and states of wonder and awe unfold. However, for the most part, our focus has been on developing our extrasensory awareness as an avenue through which we can receive helpful and practical guidance and information.

For instance, by listening within, we may be offered additional insights into our everyday decisions, choices, and challenges. Intuitive and empathic awareness can provide us with new information and options and confirmation that we are on the right track. Moments of connection with a higher source of awareness also offer us glimpses into an aspect of ourselves that lies beyond our five senses.

Although we want our extrasensory awareness to make our lives easier and more abundant and fulfilling, intuiting isn't always straightforward. It can take us down a path of twists and turns, with unexpected obstacles. Despite our best efforts to intuitively access beneficial information, we may not receive the clear and accurate insights we desire. We may be confused by the chaotic energy swirling around in our head or not receive anything at all. We may also receive too much, with a variety of feelings, images, and thoughts pouring in that we cannot make sense of.

If you have felt frustrated or discouraged by your intuitive and empathic abilities, you are not alone. Energy information doesn't follow the same rules as our logical and analytical thinking. It has its own language and may not show up in a way that makes sense. It may be absent when we need it most, then randomly emerge with clarity and precision.

Intuitive and empathic energy can be mysterious and hard to grasp and not adhere to our desires and attempts to control it and use it the way we would like. Although it may seem evasive and unpredictable, it embodies a great depth of wisdom and love. We don't have to make it do what we want or manipulate it into providing us with what we want and need. The root of intuitive and empathic awareness winds into our soul and spirit. When we explore it through these spiritual avenues, it leads us to higher forces that always operate in our highest good.

Unfortunately we often approach extrasensory awareness as if it were a foreign invader or a scary spirit presence that we must subdue and wrestle into abiding by our wishes. Instead of trying to control our extrasensory awareness, we can open our heart and mind and allow it the space to unfold naturally. Inherent within our high sensitivity and intuitive and empathic awareness is the invitation to go beyond the known and into the cosmic wonder of who we are and what is possible. The obstacles that get in the way of clear intuiting are messengers and portals pushing and leading us into a new understanding of its true potential.

Those annoying issues that seem to get in the way of intuiting and incite stress and confusion become stepping stones.

Intuition and the Chattering Mind

While we assume that we should be able to approach our intuitive and empathic ability in the same way that we go about learning and mastering other skills, tasks, and subjects, we soon discover that this doesn't work. There are long-standing and recurring obstacles that most of us encounter at one time or another. The most common challenge we seek help with is how to differentiate self-generated thoughts from intuited energy. The inability to distinguish between intuited thoughts and mind chatter can cause us to misinterpret the feelings and messages we receive. This can lead to making bad choices and decisions and becoming disillusioned and distrustful of our intuition.

When we take a moment to listen to our thoughts, we may notice that at any given moment there is a lot going on inside of us simultaneously. Along with our sensitivity and receptivity to energy, we are constantly bombarded with inner chatter. Thoughts, feelings, judgments, and opinions about ourselves, others, and random information come and go for no apparent reason. While our mind does its best to make sense of all of these stimuli, it often doesn't get very far.

The inner voices vying for our attention can make it difficult to hear and trust the subtle intuitive and empathic energy we receive. When we listen to the constant inner chatter, we often discover an inner dialogue that is always monitoring whatever we encounter and experience. Its interpretations and judgments are constantly being expressed.

The inner chatter might go something like this:

I need to stop by the store on the way home from work and pick up some things. I can't believe I forgot so much when I went grocery shopping a few days ago. Emma kept me on the phone and distracted me. She's not going to like that I don't want to go to the lake this weekend. I just don't like being around her boyfriend. He seems like he's hiding something. There's something about him that feels off to me, like he's not being honest. Or maybe I'm just jealous. I just need to get to the store and pack. I've got to accept her boyfriend.

The inner chatter might jump from thought to thought and take different perspectives. It may even argue with itself and doesn't always make much sense. We are usually too wrapped up in what is going on in our head to notice our intuitive and energy sensitivity. No matter what we experience, encounter, or feel, the voice in our head keeps talking. When we take a step back and listen, we may begin to realize that the chattering voice has something to say about everything and anything. Even though it keeps going and going, it doesn't always know what it is talking about.

The voice in our head is especially perplexed and annoyed when we experience nonphysical phenomena. If we are sure or simply suspect that we are intuiting or sensing energy information or insights, the inner chatter makes it difficult to allow this part of us to fully surface. When we become aware of an intuited thought or insight, we may initially trust what we receive and feel. However, the doubting inner voice is never far away. Whatever confidence we may have had during an emphatic or intuitive event is soon discounted and discouraged.

Here is an example:

I feel I need to call Kevin. It feels like he is going through something. Maybe I should find out if everything is okay. I feel like he is having a hard time and needs someone to talk to, but I don't want to embarrass myself if I'm wrong. I'm sure he's fine. It's probably just my imagination—always is. Why do I do this? I just need to calm down and focus. I have enough to do without coming up with stuff that makes no sense.

The inner chattering voice and our energy sensitivity are usually at odds with each other. They perceive things differently and don't agree on much of anything. It's not always easy to sort through the confusion that comes when different parts of us try to get our attention.

When our logical self and our energy sensitivity are both trying to get our attention, it might sound something like this:

I know things without knowing how I know them. I need to better understand why this is happening. How do I find out more about how to develop my intuition? I'm crazy just for thinking this. There are other, more important things I need to worry about. I know I'm an empath and sensitive to all kind of things, but how do I turn this off? Will it go away for good?

Paradoxically, as we become better at identifying intuitive energy information, we may find that our inner dialogue initially becomes more argumentative. The chattering mind will do all it can to take charge and control what we are experiencing. Inner chatter comes from our ego, and it tries all kinds of tactics to interpret and control the energy sensations and stimuli that we intuitively receive. The mind chatter doesn't pause and listen, but just keeps going and going. Throughout the day, we tend to go back and forth, taking opposing views on what we feel and experience. In this never-ending dialogue, we might identify with one of these views over the other, only to find ourself flip-flopping back and forth. It may go something like this:

> *I don't think I should take this route to work today. I know it's a bright sunny day, but that doesn't necessarily mean anything. I don't know why I feel this way. This route always gets me to where I'm going. I remember the last time I felt that there would be an issue and I went a different way. I was right—there was an accident on my usual route. Maybe I should listen to these feelings and take the back roads. But if I'm wrong, I might be late. It does take longer... Oh, forget it. I think I'll just listen to the radio. That will change my mood.*

Then just when we think we have made a reasonable decision and start listening to the radio instead of these annoying inner arguments, traffic comes to a standstill. Several minutes later, with still no movement in stuck traffic, our chattering mind goes at it again:

> *I knew not to take this route. Why don't I ever listen to these feelings? How could I know there was going to be traffic? It makes no sense.*

On and on the inner dialogue continues until our head hurts. Along with this mind chatter, we might at the same time experience an influx of intuitive knowing and sensing. It might not seem like there is a way to turn it all off. The constant back-and-forth between our chattering mind and our deeper, more intuitive and soulful knowing seems endless. Although we may try to listen to and understand our sensitivity and intuitive thoughts, the constant inner chatter can get in the way.

Even when we are comfortable with receiving and working with intuited and empathic energy, a part of us may question its validity and create doubt. When the voice in our head encounters insights and feelings that originate from outside of the domain of our five senses, it attempts to seize control. Even when we are open to intuitively sensing and feeling the energy of others and the environment, we may allow mind chatter to take over. Our awareness shifts away from being in the flow of energy awareness and into thinking mode.

We often choose to listen to the chattering mind because it is familiar and feels like an essential part of who we are. We believe that the often critical inner voice offers us protection from the world around us and the unknown. Yet when we trust and give our power to this voice, it stirs up our emotions and supports our fears. It confirms our doubts and we become more defensive and confused. In this rush of reactive emotions, we cannot sort out the origins of the feelings, sensations, and thoughts that we are experiencing. This makes it more difficult to know if we are receiving intuited energy or if what we are experiencing is self-generated. Our awareness becomes clouded and the chattering mind fills our head with what it wants us to believe. It directs our attention to more everyday concerns that we feel we can handle and successfully deal with. The energy sensitivity and intuitive awareness that triggered doubt and confusion becomes a faint memory.

We might also listen to the voice in our head's interpretation of what we intuit because we don't know what else to do. We know ourselves, others, and our environment through our thinking self. We may not be aware of an alternative. When we don't know why and what the subtle intuitive knowing and sensations mean and how to better understand what is happening, we listen to the voice that seems to know what it is talking about. However, when it comes to intuited and empathic insights and feelings, the voice in our head has no real insights or awareness to share. It is empty talk.

The following exercise will help you better differentiate intuited energy information from mind chatter.

....

EXERCISE
Tuning into the Intuitive Voice

Get comfortable and take a few long, deep inhales and relaxing exhales.

Listen within. Don't try to regulate, eliminate, or censor the thoughts in your head. Just listen without judgment.

Notice the reactions you have to your thoughts. Perhaps some thoughts invoke strong feelings and others are irritating or make you tired. Some thoughts may feel more compelling, interesting, or comforting. Allow yourself to tune into how your thoughts make you feel.

As you continue to listen within and allow your thoughts and feelings to surface, notice any thoughts that have a particular energetic quality to them. These thoughts may be accompanied by a feeling of expansion or tingling sensations on your scalp or skin or that feel like they are moving up your spine. You might feel a slight buzzing in your body or head. These thoughts and feelings may be more neutral and don't incite a strong emotion or try to convince you of anything. They are persistent and yet mild and almost matter-of-fact. These are some of the sensations that accompany intuitive receptivity.

If you feel that you are receiving intuitive energy, relax. Don't overthink or try too hard to receive or figure out what these intuitive thoughts and feelings mean. Breathe and relax and allow the energy and sensations to come and go.

Creating a more open and curious approach to intuitive and empathic awareness begins by identifying and differentiating the intuitive voice from the chattering mind. If we pay attention and focus on listening to our intuitive sensing, we notice that it is more sure of itself than we might have thought. Unlike the voice of the chattering mind, intuitive and empathic information tends to be neutral, persistent, and understated. These messages don't incite strong emotions or wave flags and try to get our attention. This is simple and calm inner awareness.

The Overwhelmed Empath

Empaths absorb and feel the emotional energy of others and the environment. We are like sponges that take the feelings, moods, and energy of others into our mind, heart, and physical body. This sensitivity is often most acute and confusing in our relationships with others. While energy sensitivity offers us the ability to gain insight and guidance about ourselves and others, we are not always able to take advantage of what we receive. When our personal feelings of love and care for another are involved, it can be challenging to sort out our feelings from our empathic receptivity. We often go back and forth between feeling the energy of our empathic sensitivity and our own feelings. Not only is this overwhelming, but we become more confused and unsure of ourselves.

For instance, here is Clara's experience:

Jeff just needs a little more love and understanding. He didn't realize that he was hurting my feelings. It's really my fault anyway, since my feelings are easily hurt. No one else seems to notice or be bothered by him. How can he stand it when I am so sensitive? When I'm with him, I become so overwhelmed with conflicting feelings. I don't always know if these are my feelings or his, but I can feel it, his hurt and pain. I wish he would let me help him. I don't know what to do. I feel that maybe I should walk away, but I love him and I can feel all of the difficulties he has been through.

When it comes to relationships, we may invalidate, discourage, and discount our emotional sensitivity. Empaths often have intense feelings, and along with our intuited emotions, we may experience an emotional overload. As much as we desire to be more aware and trust what we empathically feel, it may not always be easy to decipher and make sense of the jumble of emotions and ups and downs we experience.

An empath's nervous system can be easily triggered by the unspoken feelings and needs of others. When it becomes overly burdened, we experience higher levels of anxiety and stress. This can lead to increased feelings of worry and concern about the unhealthiness of the energy that we are absorbing and taking in, yet we may feel powerless and be embarrassed and blame ourselves for our troubling feelings. To manage our emotions, we may limit our exposure to the people and environments that seem to trigger uncomfortable feelings. We might also attempt to stop the onslaught of confusing emotions by shutting down our extrasensory receptivity, closing our heart and no longer feeling empathy for others. We might even criticize ourselves for the depth of our emotional reaction and feel a sense of shame for being different.

As an example, here is Jen's experience:

I'm not sure what I am feeling and why I feel this way. As soon as I walked into my weekly work meeting yesterday, a wave of dread flowed through me. All day something seemed to be weighing me down. Then this morning it was announced that the company is going to start laying off people in my department. I wonder if my feelings of dread and heaviness had to do with the layoffs that are being planned. Does that sound crazy? It took everyone by surprise.

After some time, Jen accepted that the emotions she was feeling were likely connected to the layoffs that were eventually announced. She then remembered that on another occasion in a past meeting, she had felt nervous and filled with apprehension about the company. When a reorganization was announced a few days later, she realized that her empathic feelings proved to be correct.

Instead of this realization being a positive affirmation of her extrasensory sensitivity, Jen was uneasy. She became concerned that she would continue to feel and absorb the energy of unfortunate events and become overwhelmed by them. She didn't want to feel emotions that didn't make any sense and not know and understand what they were connected to. Jen feared that she wouldn't be able to be happy and just feel good for any length of time. Although she was aware of the emotions she felt, she wasn't always able to adequately put into words and fully understand what it all meant.

Interpreting intuitive and empathic messages isn't always easy. We often rely too much on our analytical thinking mind to make sense of the often overwhelming energy that we absorb and intuit. Because our mind chatter seems to be able to come up with interpretations that make sense, we accept them. However, it usually filters extrasensory energy through the lens of our assumptions, expectations, needs, and desires. We tend to listen to this interpretation because we hear what we want to hear. Here is an example.

Eileen felt an unexplainable connection when first meeting Zach. Her stomach was doing somersaults and a shiver of energy ran up her spine. As an empath, she immediately felt that she *knew* Zach. The feeling that she shared a soul connection with him was uncanny and strong. The voice in her head interpreted these feelings and sensations as a sign that they could share a special love connection.

Even though her gut told her to go slow and be careful, Eileen put aside any hesitations and dove into a relationship with Zach. Wanting to believe that the intuitive sensations and feelings she had experienced when first meeting him indicated a love that was meant to be, she pushed away her apprehensions. Although there were red flags in Zach's behavior and insensitivity toward her, she ignored her concerns and made excuses for him. Eventually it was Zach who broke up with Eileen after she had endured his mistreatments for far too long. Eileen's empathic and intuitive feelings of a connection with Zach had been spot-on. However, her ego-centered thinking had interpreted the feelings and sensations as a sign that they shared a loving bond.

The instant connection we feel with another may be due to their similarity with someone from our past. Upon meeting, we intuitively feel these familiar feelings, not realizing that the bond we share with them may be one not of blissful love, but of challenges and growth. This is what happened to Eileen. The familiar feeling she experienced with Zach was connected to a past unresolved relationship. It was not indicating a harmonious bond of love. Feeling an energy connection to another doesn't necessarily mean that it will lead to the fulfilling and loving relationship we might hope for.

Over the years I've given readings to attractive, kind, and intelligent people who found themselves in a relationship that they believed was *meant to be*. Unfortunately, the energy sensitivity they experienced during the first meeting was misinterpreted. Their hopes and desires for a relationship hijacked their empathic sensations and feelings and interfered with their ability to discern and interpret what they had intuitively received. If we trust our ego to interpret our intuited feelings, then our expectations for positive outcomes may not be realized. This creates more confusion and gives us more reason not to trust our empathic awareness.

....

EXERCISE
Attuned Within

When we become confused and overwhelmed by the emotional energy that we absorb and feel from others, it can be helpful to create space and listen within. If we are preoccupied with trying to figure out what is coming to us from another versus what is self-generated, we only get more confused. If we are overly focused on another, we may try to manage their feelings and issues and disregard how their energy affects us. Being too centered on another and what we can do for them creates a disconnect with our sense of self and our power.

If you are feeling confused and overwhelmed with empathic feelings, try this.

Get comfortable and take some long, deep, relaxing breaths. Exhale any stress and tension. Tune into your body and feel any tension and tightness, then release this through the exhale.

Listen within and allow any feelings or thoughts to surface. Don't try to figure out what they mean or who or where they are coming from.

As you breathe and relax, focus on an emotion as it surfaces. If you become aware of more than one emotion, focus on the one that feels the strongest. Do your best to name this emotion or feeling.

Notice if the emotion or feeling becomes faint and begins to dissipate as you breathe, acknowledge it, and name it. This is a sign that you have likely intuited this emotion. Don't try to figure out its significance. Breathe and let it go.

You are safe, and the energy and emotions you receive from others or outer influences do not have power over you and cannot harm you.

Notice if the emotion or feeling gets stronger and you feel it more intensely in your body as you breathe and name it. If this happens, it is likely a self-generated emotion.

Listen to this emotion and pay attention to any insights or messages that it offers you. If the emotion is uncomfortable or difficult, you can also ask it what it needs to feel love.

Continue to breathe and name the emotions as they surface.

Eventually your heart, mind, and being will relax and your inner harmony will be restored.

One of the common responses we have when we experience overwhelming feelings is to try to protect ourselves. The root of our tendency to feel that we are at the mercy of the energy of others and the environment lies in our belief that we are powerless. We don't know how to contend with the intangible something within us that responds to and receives this energy. When we are affected and influenced by what appear to be outer forces that our five senses and our analytical mind cannot control, we may become fearful.

The remedy for our empathic distress is within us. As we form a better understanding of our relationship with our heart and spirit, we reclaim our power. Our empathic awareness isn't meant to be a source of discomfort and fear and feeling overwhelmed. Instead, it can be an oasis of harmony and pure love that nourishes our deepest needs and calms our worries and stress.

The Highly Sensitive Person's Disbelief

Those of us who are highly sensitive don't always consider ourselves intuitive or empathic. Instead, we are focused on the material world of the five senses. Such things as noise, scents, bright lights, and crowds of people can be overstimulating and overwhelming. The highly sensitive often focus on controlling and negotiating the stimulation of the outer world. We don't necessarily perceive that what we are experiencing is coming from our empathic and intuitive nature. Although we feel, sense, and are influenced by the energy of others and the environment, we might deny and disbelieve that this is possible. We may not attribute what we are experiencing to anything other than environmental and nervous system overstimulation. The thought of being sensitive to energy that is not attached to the material realm might not make sense. Doing our best to stay focused on day-to-day concerns and worries, we don't give intuitive and empathic insights and sensations much attention.

Even if we find the idea of intuiting and feeling nonphysical energy to be intriguing, we may try to rationalize and deny that we are able to receive energy from nonphysical sources. If we have a clear experience of extrasensory awareness, we may find reasons to dismiss it. For many, the suggestion or hint that they may be empathic or intuitive is quickly dismissed.

Here is Emmy's experience. Maybe you can relate.

This party is overwhelming. There are too many people and too much noise. I thought it would be fun, but now I just want to leave. But it's important to Jennifer that everyone has a good time. I can feel her anxiousness and don't want to disappoint her. It would hurt her if I looked like I wasn't enjoying myself. Why am I such a baby, anyway? I just need to mingle and talk to some people. I feel so much stress in this room. It's all too overwhelming, and I just want to go home. My God, can I ever just get over it? I need a drink. People are going to think I'm strange. Why do I always have to be the most sensitive one in the room?

Highly sensitive individuals may attribute all of their overwhelming feelings and sensations to outer physical stimuli. While we are affected by noise, crowds, smells, and even the lighting in a room, we are also likely to take in the energy vibes of people and the environment. Unfortunately, many feel a sense of shame and embarrassment for being uncomfortable and unable to handle what others seem to be unaffected by.

We often unknowingly absorb the energy of others and our environment into our physical body. This is one of the reasons we may not believe that we are intuitive. We don't receive empathic energy through common extrasensory channels, such as images, knowing, or hearing. Because we tend to feel energy as physical sensations, we deny and refute any other possibility. If we are in a stressful situation or with others who are going through difficulties, we may feel this as a headache, nausea, or tightness throughout our body. Rarely do we realize that physical sensations and aches and pains may be coming from intuited energy. Sometimes just thinking about another can create physical stress and aches and pains. When we experience a gut feeling or vibe or a tingle of energy or when an undefined feeling suddenly comes over us, doubt and denial surface.

Maybe this experience sounds familiar:

I'm looking forward to going out to dinner with Michelle. I like connecting with her and catching up on what's been going on in her life. It's strange, though, that it seems like my back hurts when I think about seeing her. Maybe I'm making this up and it's just a coincidence. I wonder sometimes if she talks about me to others. There's a weird feeling in my gut telling me that I can't trust her. I want to trust her and I like her, but she's had a lot to deal with. Isn't this what being a friend is, though, just accepting her as she is? Now my neck is starting to hurt.

It is challenging to be highly sensitive and live in our loud and constantly in motion world. Many deny and don't want to consider the possibility that they are empathic or intuitive because it is just too much to deal with. Contending with the physical world is enough of a chore. Trying to negotiate hard-to-detect energy sources that may be influencing and affecting us is just too overwhelming to consider.

If we do acknowledge that we may be empathic and intuitive, we may go back and forth between being open and curious about it and feeling silly for believing in the validity of what we feel and sense. However, when we deny its existence, we may not be aware of when we receive energy information.

Here are a few examples:

I think I can feel what my friend Lacey is feeling and going through. She doesn't want to talk about it, but I can feel her pain and confusion. Oh, who am I kidding? How would I know what she's feeling? I can't let things like this bother me so much. It just gives me a headache.

When I pass the homeless encampments, my heart aches. It feels like I absorb this heavy and stressful energy. I've started to go a different way to work. It's just too overwhelming.

I feel so much sadness when I'm near one of my coworkers. We're not close and it's a work situation, so I can't bring this up to her and ask her about it. How can I feel someone else's feelings though? That can't be possible. I've got to get to bed earlier. Maybe I'm just tired and making all this up.

How do I figure out how to control my feelings and not let everything affect me so much? It's just too draining. I need to remember to limit the stimuli I'm exposed to and my contact with others.

I think I feel and know things that others aren't aware of. If I told anyone this, they would think I was crazy. I probably am. I'm so delusional.

When we deny and don't accept that we may be receiving energy and vibes from others, we become disconnected from our own feelings and needs. We miss the opportunity for further self-awareness and the possibility of receiving helpful insights and messages. Even when we successfully shut down, deny, or rationalize our energy sensitivity, it is only temporary.

However much we may try to protect ourselves from energy, it exists everywhere and is in all things. This will never change. We may try to avoid those things and activities that trigger sensations and uncomfortable and unexplained feelings. Still, our empathic and intuitive receptivity follows its own laws and cannot be subdued or made to conform to our version of what is possible. It continues to be what it is, despite our denial and disbelief. Eventually, intuited and empathic feelings, thoughts, and sensations resurface.

Here is Kate's experience:

There's something about Jerry that feels off to me. I don't know what it is. This weird feeling crawls up my spine and I feel like I need to get away from him, but then I think I've got to stop being so sensitive. Just because he's a little different doesn't mean there's something off with him. But still, it doesn't feel right to ignore this weird feeling. I don't know what to do. He seems nice enough though. Maybe I'll accept his dinner invitation. It would be nice to go out. He's got a great job and he is good-looking. It wouldn't hurt to get to know him better. Maybe it's just my nerves. I haven't been on a date in a while.

When we are aware of our intuitive and empathic abilities, we are more willing to pay attention to the unexpected feelings and vibes and uncomfortable energy we experience with others. When we deny that this is possible, we ignore the helpful and sometimes protective energy we receive.

....

EXERCISE
Am I an Empath?

If you're not sure if you are intuitive, empathic, and/or highly sensitive, try this.

When you notice a sensation in your physical body or feel an emotion or have an insight that seems to come out of nowhere, write it down. Don't try to figure it out or overthink it, and don't be overly concerned about whether it is coming from a known or an unknown source. Just write it down. You might also want to include the date and what is going on in your life at this time.

Continue to notice and record these kinds of questionable episodes and experiences. Resist looking back at what you wrote right away. After a few weeks and/or many entries, take a look at what you wrote. Notice any patterns and connections to anything that was going on in your life during and after the experiences.

When we give our extrasensory experiences space to unfold without trying to understand them right away, clarity and new insights emerge.
....

The Message within Common Obstacles

Some common obstacles that most of us confront when intuiting include interference from the chattering mind, difficulty differentiating energy information from self-generated thoughts and feelings, feeling overwhelmed with energy, denying our extra-sensory abilities, and fear that the energy we are absorbing may be negative or unhealthy. We may struggle with some of these challenges more than others, yet we all experience these issues to some degree.

While we may devise ways and methods to circumvent and work through these obstacles to clear intuiting, our attempts are somewhat limited. Even when we experience more clarity and improvement in our ability to receive and interpret energy infor-mation, it may still be elusive and not as accurate and helpful as we'd like. We want to use our intuition to improve all areas of our lives. It would be self-sabotaging and silly to want anything else. However, our assumptions about how to get the best from our empathic and intuitive awareness get in the way.

All of the obstacles to more accurate and rewarding intuit-ing arise from ego domination and a lack of connection to and conscious alignment with our spirit. We approach intuitive and empathic energy through overthinking and our expectations, fears, and desires. Our inability to differentiate absorbed and intuited energy from the chattering mind reminds us that we have put our ego self in charge of our extrasensory awareness. While the ego is an essential and healthy part of our functioning, it cannot fully understand the subtleties of energy. The ego may be aware of who we are in the physical, mental, and emotional realms, yet it doesn't have access to our spirit and extrasensory abilities. It may understand these things as theories, ideas, and thoughts, but it doesn't interact with and experience our spirit.

The difficulties we experience with differentiating intuited insights from self-generated thoughts come from our attempts to control and better understand what we are receiving through overthinking. When we try to decipher energy information through a purely logical and analytical mindset, we experience confusion and doubt.

Being overwhelmed with energy provides us with the awareness that we embody a high degree of energy sensitivity. This insight speaks to our potential for extrasensory mastery. It is a message to further explore our spiritual nature and become familiar with our gifts.

Too often we project the limitations that we experience in the physical and material realm onto the boundlessness of energy. We think that because something isn't materially possible, it is also out-of-bounds and not feasible in the spirit realm. Fear of the unknown and our inability to control empathic and intuitive energy keep us from experiencing the rich, creative abundance that is our birthright.

The voice of the chattering mind, fueled by the ego, is convincing, while our spirit appears to be meek and barely detectable. We don't always recognize the finer whisperings of our heart and spirit and may lack an awareness of the spiritual forces that reside within us.

Adopt the beginner's mind and accept that overthinking and trying to figure out and control our extrasensory awareness doesn't work. When we open our heart and listen within to our spirit, the divine interpretation of our intuitive and empathic awareness is revealed. We aren't confused by the chattering voice, as we realize that it has no real power. There is no fear of becoming overwhelmed by another's negativity or unhealthy energy. We are able to choose the energy that we absorb and cannot be influenced by forces that are not in our highest good. We are aligned with our power and connected to beneficial higher frequencies of energy.

As we move beyond finite thinking, we draw closer to and become more aware of the gifts of extrasensory awareness. The infinite potential and expressions of energy extend far beyond our material obstacles and understanding. The higher vibrations of energy frequency are fueled by pure divine life force energy and encompass love, goodness, and creative abundance. Our spirit resides in this higher frequency. As we open our heart and attune to our spirit, we naturally receive the good of the higher realms.

Our spiritual challenge is to go beyond our assumptions about our intuitive and empathic sensitivity and our need to control it. When we begin to perceive the possibilities and potential of our energy sensitivity, we begin to align with our spirit and unlock our power. As we practice new ways of working in unison with energy, we discover that the spirit realm wants what we want: abundance, love, and all good things.

In the next chapter, we draw closer to our spirit through listening within, with curiosity and an open mind and heart.

CHAPTER 3

Refining Our Inner Senses

Energy sensitivity is a powerful gift and ally. We are rarely able to fully understand its significance, as we are too busy trying to figure it out and making assumptions about what it is and isn't. The voices in our head cannot help us. To know truth, we often have to give up wanting and trying to find it. The spiritual path is a paradox. Sometimes the most powerful action we can take is to be comfortable with not knowing and not having the answers. When we accept the mystery, the voices in our head begin to lose their power. They will still try to get our attention and lure us into relying on their input, but they will not be as attractive as they once were. We are better able to resist being pulled into the useless chatter. When we let go of trying to understand the meaning of what we intuitively and empathically receive, we are better able to hear the whispers of truth.

To muffle the constant inner activity of ego chatter, become the observer. Notice your thoughts and emotions without reacting to them or trying to understand what is happening. The voices in our head are fueled by our desires, fears, and expectations. Because of this, we believe what our inner chatter tells us and give it our power. Take a step back and detach from the chattering mind. Notice the constant inner dialogue that goes on and on. It doesn't matter if you are busy and involved in activities or quiet and alone; the inner chatter is always present. Observe this inner activity without getting involved in it. From this state of being, you can observe without becoming intertwined in the chaos within and around you.

As we listen to our inner dialogue, we may notice that some of what is going on within feels good and some might not feel so good. We might want to identify with the good thoughts and reject the not-so-good ones. Yet we aren't our thoughts, even the pleasant ones. We are the one who is aware of them. Notice that when emotions are triggered, the inner dialogue gets stronger and louder and a cycle of ups and downs begins. The voices become suspicious and more judgmental. If we are excited, frustrated, or angry, the conversation in our head intensifies. When we are inwardly calm, the thoughts are more positive and the happiness we desire begins to shine through our heart and mind.

At the height of the good thoughts and feelings, unexpected worries and stress often surface. The chattering voice intrudes and lets us know that everything might not be as rosy as it appears to be. It tells us that something unexpected might happen and ruin everything. The good feelings begin to dissipate. We imagine all of the issues and problems that might arise. We can go from feeling positive to feeling anxious and worried in a short period of time, yet nothing has changed or happened. These feelings are fleeting and come and go. When we take our mind chatter too seriously, we are tossed and turned and left confused and pulled into the inner turmoil. Instead of listening to the thoughts and opinions of the chattering mind and believing what these voices are telling us, practice detachment. When positive and good feelings go back and forth with the stressful and worrisome thoughts, we can remind ourselves that we are not our thoughts. Instead, we can ask ourselves: Who are these voices talking to? Who is doing the talking and who is listening?

Observe and let the thoughts, feelings, and judgments rattle on without reacting. When we approach the inner dialogue of the chattering mind with curiosity, a space opens up for new awareness.

··

MEDITATION
Allow Energy to Flow

Take a moment to observe what is happening within. Don't engage the thinking mind. Instead, sit quietly and breathe. Allow feelings and thoughts to move through you without assigning meaning to what you experience.

When you begin to feel the chattering mind trying to get your attention and rattle on about all kinds of things, take a long, deep inhale and a relaxing exhale.

Observe the chattering voice as it continues to try and pull you into its dialogue. Pause and focus on the breath, and exhale any stress and tension. Continue to breathe and move the energy of the breath through your body.

Allow any emotions that surface to move through you without attaching to them. Observe any sensations, movement, or stress and tension in the body. Notice the thoughts and sensations without overthinking them, and remain open to whatever flows in. Do your best to let go and just continue to observe without trying to give meaning to what you are experiencing.

When we observe and don't react to or engage with our thoughts, whatever we receive moves through us. We don't attach and hold onto it.

Notice the observer within you—the quiet, still awareness that notices the thoughts, feelings, sensations, and intuitive and empathic energy.

Allow whatever flows in to move through you.
....

Questions for Clarity

When we don't engage with our thoughts and emotions, it become easier to notice intuitive and empathic energy as it surfaces. Quite often we slip into intuitive knowing, feeling, and sensing when we least expect it. We may be at work, driving down the highway, doing chores, or involved in other activities when empathic and intuited messages, sensations, and feelings emerge.

If you suspect that you are receiving energy information, breathe and relax. Try not to overthink what you are receiving or engage with the inner chatter. If you focus on the meaning and significance of what you are experiencing, you may become confused and begin to feel overwhelmed. Then you will no longer be able to observe. If you believe that you are receiving an empathic and intuitive feeling, insight, or sense of knowing, breathe and ask yourself these or similar questions:

- Is the voice in my head attempting to judge, define, and assign meaning to the energy I am receiving?
- Can I let this energy flow through me without trying to figure out what it means?
- Is the voice in my head attempting to create doubt or overthink and interfere with what I am receiving?

If you feel that you are receiving energy information but are not able to differentiate intuitive energy from the chattering mind, take a deep inhale and then slowly exhale. Focus on your breath. Allow any sensations or feelings to emerge. Even if this feels uncomfortable and your mind starts to race, continue to focus on the breath. Observe what thoughts, feelings, and sensations surface without trying to understand their meaning. Give space to what is happening without engaging the thinking mind. When we focus on the breath, the inner chatter begins to subside and we gain more clarity on what we are experiencing.

It can take continued observation and practice to be able to tell the difference between our self-generated thoughts and intuitive and empathic knowing, messages, and thoughts. Much of the energy that we spontaneously intuit and feel from others is intertwined with our logical and analytical thinking. This makes it easy for the chattering mind to hijack what we intuitively receive and misinterpret it. Because the ego isn't able to understand the true meaning and significance of empathic and intuitive energy, our interpretation is often inaccurate.

When we don't overthink and jump to judgments and conclusions, we receive more clarity. For instance, when Carrie walked into a meeting with her supervisor, she felt a stressful energy in the room. Her boss didn't say anything unusual or alarming, but Carrie could feel that something was off. She was sure that there was something he was keeping to himself. She wondered if anyone else could feel his stressful vibes.

Carrie began to worry that the energy she was sensing in her supervisor's office was a message that she was going to be fired or laid off. She became increasingly stressed at the thought of being unemployed and worried about what might happen if she wasn't able to pay her bills.

Then she caught herself and realized that she was interpreting what she was intuiting and feeling through the fears of her ego. Instead of continuing to listen to the inner chatter, she took a few deep breaths and began to relax. She focused on her breath and allowed the stressful energy to flow through her.

As she observed the energy and resisted jumping to conclusions, she felt an inner assurance that everything was going to be okay. This feeling came as a quiet inner knowing, and she trusted it. Although she didn't know the significance and meaning of what she felt with her supervisor, she knew that it didn't have anything to do with her.

Carrie was correct when she intuited stressful energy in her supervisor's office. She later discovered that he was going though a difficult divorce at the time that she had intuited his tense energy.

Allowing energy to flow through us without engaging our thoughts and emotions isn't easy to do. We are subconsciously wired to try to understand and give meaning to whatever we experience. This is especially true when it comes to the unknown. There are different pathways through which self-generated thoughts and emotions and energy from an outer source make their way to our nervous system. The energy of our thoughts and emotions is known and familiar, even when those thoughts and emotions are more intense. This isn't true of intuited and absorbed energy. It is unfamiliar and sets off triggers in our deeper sensing. Because of this, we pay more attention to it and innately approach it with caution.

When our emotions don't get stirred up and we stay in a neutral state, the energy moves through us. If we react with fear, stress, or anxiety, the chattering mind jumps in. When we don't attach and offer no resistance to our inner activity, we remain clear and open. Our willingness to observe the inner drama allows our true nature to emerge. As we listen within, we discover that we aren't our thoughts or feelings. We are the quiet observer. Reminding ourselves of this takes us into the depths of our being, where a powerful journey is unfolding.

Offering No Resistance

The awareness that we are intuiting or absorbing energy might stir up our fears and apprehension about the unknown. We don't know what to do and may worry that we are absorbing negative or unhealthy energy. When we can't figure out what we are receiving and where it is coming from, we often become uncertain and even fearful. The voice in our head comes to the rescue and tries to interpret what we are experiencing. Sometimes the voice of the ego is dramatic and interprets and judges what we are intuiting through a clouded lens of the worst-case scenario. If we are uncomfortable with the unknown and unseen or are wary of what we may be energetically absorbing, we can unknowingly project these feelings onto the intuited energy.

For instance, as you quietly listen within, an unexpected empathic feeling, thought, or sensation might drift into your awareness. Your first thought might be: Why am I receiving this? Am I absorbing someone else's energy? What do these sensations mean?

The voice in your head might jump in and come up with an explanation. It might tell you that these feelings indicate that there is a problem or concern or that there is something going on in a relationship. This stirs up anxious feelings, and you begin to think about the people in your life who might somehow be connected to the intuited energy you are receiving. As you go through various possibilities, you begin to wonder if a friend or family member is upset with you. Then on and on your chattering mind goes.

When our emotions, doubts, and fears are heightened, it doesn't always feel possible to observe or direct our attention away from the chattering mind and our worries and stress. If it feels too difficult to be aware of anything other than the rambling chatter of doubts and fears, just listen. Sit quietly and listen to the constant dialogue. Let it say whatever it wants to say without getting pulled into the drama. If you offer no resistance and allow the thoughts and emotions to rattle on without reacting to them, eventually the chatter will lose its power.

Instead of overthinking and questioning what you are receiving, recognize that the voice of the ego is taking over. The insight and awareness we desire cannot be found in the inner chatter. Engaging in the constant back-and-forth of thoughts pushes us further away from the understanding we seek.

Here are some telltale signs that the chattering mind is taking over:

- The feelings and emotions that we receive create inner tension and stress.
- We have a need to understand the intuitive feelings, thoughts, and insights as they stream in. Not knowing what they mean creates stress and we may feel overwhelmed.
- We become anxious, fearful, or worried about what we are receiving.
- We feel special, like we are better or more deserving than others.

Noticing when our overthinking and emotional responses are interfering with the intuitive and empathic awareness that we seek helps us to further refine our senses. It is only when we steer our attention away from the chaos and activity of our ego responses and to the observer within that we can become aware of spiritual presence.

Intuitive and empathic awareness and our spirit are intricately and naturally connected. Our spirit most often makes itself known through the quiet expansiveness of an open heart. Unfortunately, the loud and persistent voice of our ego often seizes our attention and obstructs our ability to feel safe enough to open our heart and feel. Being comfortable with the quiet and not knowing runs counter to our normal way of doing things. To our thinking and emotional brain, silence is empty and hollow. It has no meaning and nothing to offer us. We are restless with it and prefer the ego voice, which always seems to offer us an explanation and interpretation of what we are receiving and feeling. Our innate drive to want to understand and give meaning to the intuited and empathic energy that we receive is strong. We have become accustomed to listening to and trusting the chattering mind's judgments and interpretations.

When we allow our heart to open to our intuitive and empathic awareness, we can become more conscious of our spirit's interpretation of what we are receiving. Unlike the ego, our spirit is loving and wise and doesn't make itself known through overt activity or by trying to convince us of anything. It is often still and subtle.

Becoming Aware of Vibrational Frequency

The clarity that we seek comes from listening deeper within to our heart and spirit. As we continue to observe the inner chatter, it becomes easier to notice how the ego mind is constantly monitoring and judging whatever we are experiencing. Listening to the chattering mind halts the intuitive process, while observing strengthens our ability to better discern and receive the message of what we are intuiting.

As an example, at the height of the Covid-19 pandemic, I was scheduled for a colonoscopy. Because of the threat of infection, many similar procedures were being canceled and rescheduled. I was surprised that the facility where the procedure was taking place was still operating. Although I thought of canceling just to be safe from Covid, I didn't.

For several months I had been hearing a little voice within say, "Get a colonoscopy." This persistent message didn't feel like a red flag warning and didn't incite stress or tension. It was just a little, quiet voice saying, "Get a colonoscopy."

When I thought of canceling, the voice returned. So instead, I confirmed the appointment.

When I woke up after the procedure, the doctor told me that they had removed a polyp of a type that often becomes cancerous. I was thankful that I had listened to this quiet voice.

When we open our heart and listen within to our spirit, our intuitive knowing, thoughts, and feelings are neutral, matter-of-fact, and persistent and rarely create stress or tension. When we allow ourselves the inner space to listen, we are less anxious and reactive. As the energy unfolds, we are able to become more aware of who or what these sensations are connected to. The message within the energy naturally unfolds. Even when the message is a warning, as in my case with the colonoscopy, our spirit doesn't stir up anxiety and cause us to worry.

We often don't receive the kind of information and interpretation that we believe we need and want from our intuitive and empathic awareness. When this happens, it is best to let it go. Once we accept that what we need to know comes to us without our trying to make it happen, we create the space for new insights and guidance. Receiving the meaning and message behind empathic and intuitive insights, sensations, feelings, and awareness is a bit like showing my cat affection. If I try to pet her or get her to sit on my lap, she flees. However, when I act disinterested and go about my day, she follows me around and seeks me out.

There is a wisdom and grace in higher guidance that often provides us only with what we need to know, step-by-step. Our role isn't to control and manipulate intuited energy to fulfill our desires, but to flow with it and trust its unfolding. Observing and feeling energy and sensations without attachment allows the meaning and significance of what we are experiencing to emerge without engaging the ego mind.

Not all of the intuited energy that we sense, feel, and receive is worthy of our attention. The energy that we empathically absorb from others and the environment can be negative and toxic. Even if we are patient with the process of understanding and deriving meaning and messages from what we intuit, some of what we receive has little to offer us. Some energy doesn't provide insights or clear guidance for our highest good. Instead, it can lead to confusion and fatigue and cause us to feel overwhelmed, sad, and negative. Some intuited energy is better left to simply move through us.

Observing the energy that we empathically receive can help us differentiate positive and helpful energy from energy that isn't in our highest good. As we observe, we become aware of the subtleties and distinctive vibrations and frequencies of energy.

Although many things in the physical world appear to be solid, all that we encounter is made up of vibrating energy. When energy vibrates at a slow, dense rate, it is aligned with the frequency of physicality. Our self-generated thoughts, the chattering mind, and the ego self are integrated within the denser vibration of the physical realm. The frequency of intuited energy and empathic feelings varies and is dependent on the source of the energy. Low-vibration intuited energy comes from low-vibration sources, such as negative or angry people or chaotic situations. Higher frequencies are derived from such things as loving and positive people and divine spiritual sources.

As we become more accustomed to observing and allowing energy to flow through us, we begin to notice how the frequencies and vibrations of our thoughts and feelings and our intuitive and empathic sensitivity differ.

For instance, worry, stress, and fear are often felt in the body as tension and tightness, especially in the neck, chest, and throat. These states of mind may give us headaches or muscle aches or cause digestive issues. An optimistic frame of mind and loving self-talk both have a higher frequency. Our body is more relaxed, we sleep better, and our immune system is strengthened.

Becoming aware of the frequency and vibration of our thoughts, emotions, and spirit helps us to refine our senses. As we learn the intuitive language of our spirit, essence, and energy, we are better able to identify the vibration of what we feel and absorb. With this awareness, we are able to choose to further open ourselves to positive energy or to set limits on our exposure to lower-vibration energy. Just the intent to only receive and absorb energy that is in our highest good establishes a spiritual boundary. We are powerful spiritual beings, and energy responds to our request.

....

EXERCISE
Observing Energy Frequency and Vibration

Along with observing the energy that flows into your awareness, become aware of its vibration and frequency.

Take a moment to pay attention to the thoughts and feelings swirling around within you. Let them stream through you without reacting or responding to them. Notice the self-talk, judgments, criticisms, and desires and the constant inner commentary.

Notice these thoughts and feelings, and become aware of any sensations associated with them. Some of the thoughts and emotions might feel positive and empowering. They may fill you with energy, hope, and creative inspiration. These feelings are higher in vibration and nurture us with healthy vital life energy.

Other thoughts and feelings may feel heavy or cause us to be emotionally down or feel fatigued and tired. These kinds of feelings are indications of lower-vibration energy. This energy has little to offer, so let them go through the breath.

As you breathe and become aware of the subtle vibration of your thoughts and feelings, allow them to move through you.

Take a long, deep breath, exhaling any stress or tension. Notice any sensations, feelings, and thoughts that emerge, but don't become attached to them. Maintain an open state of receptivity and continue to breathe.

In this open and receptive state, imagine breathing in white-light energy and sending it to your heart. Continue to breathe in white-light energy, and allow it to open your heart through the exhale.

Become soft and open, and flow with the vibrations that emanate from your heart. Invite the higher frequencies of wisdom and love to flow into your heart.

Sensations and feelings such as tingling, lightness, and a sense of peace indicate higher-vibration energy. Breathe in these feelings and listen within for the quiet voice of divine presence.

As you continue to observe, tune into the finer vibrations associated with the energy that moves into and from your heart.

Observing our inner activity allows moments of calm, expansive, and heart-centered space to emerge. This awareness might be fleeting and difficult to hold onto. Practice allowing these moments of openness to come and go and dissipate. Don't try to hold onto this spaciousness, and resist the temptation to overthink and try to make sense of what is happening.

Continue to breathe, relax, and observe until the awareness subsides.

Clearing Absorbed Energy

As we identify the frequency and vibration of the energy we intuit and feel, we begin to notice the different ways it influences and affects us. Through empathic awareness and high sensitivity, we often absorb the emotional and thought energy of others and the environment into our body. We may experience the energy of others and the environment as mild sensations such as the shivering of the hairs on our neck or arms, a slight headache, pressure in or on our body, or a feeling of butterflies in our gut. The energy we absorb may feel more intense. We may experience such things as a heaviness in our chest, a shortness of breath, or feelings of stress and panic.

At times we may be aware of when we feel and sense another's energy and receive empathic feelings and random sensations, but not always. It isn't always easy to untangle absorbed energy and sensing from our own feelings and aches and pains. It may not occur to us until later that what we felt or sensed came to us through our empathic sensitivity.

For instance, here is Claire's experience:

I was texting my friend Kandace and all of a sudden I felt this burst of energy in my chest. Then this weird vibration started to move into my gut. I wondered if this was a muscle spasm, but I didn't have any pain.

Kandace is on her way to Bali, and when I think of her, my head feels like it's expanding. She's going on a yoga and meditation retreat. It feels like it's going to be powerful. These strange sensations and feelings started when she told me that she was thinking of attending this retreat. Why am I feeling this energy? What does it mean? Maybe it's her energy. She's so excited.

Sometimes the energy we empathically absorb and feel is intense and overwhelming. We don't know why we are absorbing these vibrations or what to do about them. They are in sharp contrast to the more neutral and calming emotional energy that emerges from within our heart and spirit. If the energy that we empathically absorb feels negative or uncomfortable, we may become fearful or concerned. We may worry that it is detrimental to our well-being and may cause us harm in some way. Our need to protect ourselves from what feels like toxic or negative energy becomes a priority.

If you feel like you have absorbed energy that you would like to release or like you are prone to absorbing and taking in the energy of others and the environment, you are not alone. This is a concern for many. When we feel that we are susceptible to outer energy influences, our tendency is to shut down. We might do our best to avoid or muffle our intuitive and empathic receptivity. However, when we get into a fearful or defensive mode, we can't access the higher energy vibrations.

Even though our instinct is to protectively pull our energy in, it is our open heart that offers relief and energetic safety. Darkness flees from the light. Positive, loving, high vibrations lift us above and out of reach of lower, heavier energy.

EXERCISE
The Open Heart of Protection

When you feel the need to guard against external forces and the energy of others, try this.

Inhale white-light energy down through the top of your head. Send this energy throughout your entire being. Exhale any stress and tension.

Continue taking long, deep white-light inhales, and exhale any stress and tension in the body. When you feel more relaxed, imagine inhaling white light and exhaling this energy through the heart.

Continue to inhale white light and exhale through the heart. As you exhale, imagine your heart opening like a flower, petal by petal.

As your heart opens, invite the power and presence of high-vibration spiritual presence to flow through you and surround you with white light.

Imagine the blossoming of light within your heart. Allow this energetic essence to move through your being.

In harmony with your breath, this high-vibration energy moves through you and releases and clears any energy within and surrounding you that is not in your highest good.

Continue to inhale white-light energy and exhale through your heart. Allow the essence of light to cleanse and clear your physical body and extend into your energy field that surrounds you.

As you absorb the light into your being, you may want to say a short prayer of protection, such as this:

May the light of the divine flowing from my heart surround me, my home, my pets, and my loved ones and fully and completely cleanse and clear any lower vibrations that are not in my highest good.

Divine energy vibrates at a high rate of frequency. This frequency is not limited to time and space and is not subject to the laws of physicality. Our spirit, the true and eternal part of us, is non-physical and can access these higher frequencies. This energy may create noticeable sensations as it flows into our being. We may feel a buzzing or tingling sensation or a feeling of expansion in the head, heart, or other parts of our body. A shiver of energy might run up our spine or we might feel lightheaded. Sparkles and flashes of light or purple, magenta, green, white, or gold energy might appear, and random images and visions might also surface. Divine guidance naturally flows into our awareness. Embodying higher frequencies expands our awareness and allows for the manifestation of our highest good.

There is a vast landscape within us to explore. Although we are usually focused on the activity of our finite thinking brain and our emotional responses, we are so much more than that. As we become more familiar with our spiritual aspects, we discover loving, wise, and powerful forces directed toward our highest good.

The spiritual challenge is to observe our inner chatter and activity and the intuitive and empathic energy as it flows through us. Instead of listening to the ego mind and trying to control our intuitive and empathic receptivity, we open our heart to the powerful presence of our spirit.

Taking a step back and observing both the chattering mind and the intuitive voice as it flows into our awareness is a powerful spiritual step in our awakening to our truth. We are no longer confined to a purely physical orientation. As we allow energy to flow through us without engaging the chattering mind, the lighter intangible presence within emerges. This is spiritual consciousness.

PART II
Consciousness

CHAPTER 4

Who Am I?

The voices in our head that vie for our attention and seem to be opposed to one another stem from our multidimensional being. The chattering mind sometimes seems to make sense, and sometimes it is chaotic and creates an inner tension and stress. This is also true of our intuitive and empathic sensitivity. At times what we intuitively feel, sense, know, and experience provides valuable insights and guidance, while at other times it feels confusing and nonsensical.

When we practice observing the activity going on in our head, detaching from its constant inner dialogue becomes easier. Once we begin to realize that we are not our thoughts or the intuitive energy we absorb and feel, we may wonder, "Who am I? What within me is doing the observing?"

We usually perceive just small aspects and snippets of who we are. For instance, in various types of social and work-related settings, we may be asked to share more about ourselves. Our answer usually depends on who is doing the asking. In social situations, we might share with others how we spend our time and our interests, hobbies, and background. In a professional setting, we might choose to share more information about our occupation, work life, and accomplishments. A doctor might see us in terms of our height, weight, cholesterol levels, blood pressure numbers, and other physical characteristics.

Most people know us in a way that makes sense to them. Although the characteristics by which others define us may be factually correct, these aspects of our nature may not reveal much of who we really are.

Not only do others describe and know us in various ways, but this is how we know ourselves. On any given day, our sense of who we are may change. This shifting of self-awareness is dependent on many factors. Our changing thoughts, emotions, and physical health all contribute to and influence who we believe ourselves to be. External factors and our thoughts, feelings, and beliefs may shift from one moment to the next, changing our self-perception. Societal and cultural norms and expectations also contribute to how we view ourselves. From a young age, we receive overt and silent messages about our physical appearance, intelligence, and abilities. Most of the characteristics by which we define ourselves may be factually and logically true, yet this truth is relative or temporary. Our occupation, hair color, weight, opinions, likes and dislikes, and other defining characteristics are not necessarily long-lasting.

However, there are times when we catch a glimpse of the part of us that cannot be defined in a worldly, physical, or logical way. For instance, one of the surprises of getting older is that we begin to notice that the "I" inside of us doesn't seem to age. Even though there is tangible evidence that we are aging, there is a part of us that looks in the mirror and wonders why we look so old. We don't necessarily identify with that older us staring back in the mirror. Consciousness is ageless and always in present time.

Immediately after passing over, we may view ourselves from outside of our physical body. During medium sessions, my clients often express concern that their loved ones experienced pain and suffering when they passed over. However, I've never had a soul tell me that dying was painful. Once the soul begins to leave the physical body, we no longer feel pain. The awareness of self shifts from being a physical being under the laws of the material world to being a spirit and soul. This shift in awareness allows us entry into a dimension where there is no pain or suffering.

Being emphatic, intuitive, and highly sensitive opens a door through which we can better feel, know, and experience ourselves beyond the physical body and five senses. This intangible presence and awareness within us is our consciousness. It is through consciousness that we are aware of both our internal self, such as our thoughts, feelings, dreams, and intuitive sensing, and the outer world, such as our physical environment and the information that our five senses provides us. Consciousness is the wholeness of our existence that cannot be fully known or understood through words and thoughts. Becoming aware of ourselves in this way is an evolutionary step into a new way of being.

The View from Our Level of Consciousness

We generally inhabit three levels of consciousness: material, mental, and spiritual. Each level of consciousness offers a distinct perspective of reality. It defines how we experience the world and ourselves. The quality of our day-to-day life, the limitations we encounter, and the amount of abundance and joy that flow into our lives are determined by our level of consciousness. The energy that we intuit, feel, and sense is also determined by our level of consciousness. As we ascend into higher states of consciousness, our intuitive and empathic sensitivity transforms.

To better understand these three different levels of consciousness, imagine standing on a street in a city or other populated area. Likely we see buildings, people, cars, and a lot of activity. We may hear the honking of horns, people speaking to one another, and the distant drone of constant activity. There are people going about their day, and there is a general feeling of busyness. The air is filled with the exhaust fumes of traffic and the scents of food cooking from nearby restaurants and the odor of garbage. There is so much to take in, and our attention is focused on the activity, sounds, smells, and people around us.

When we stand on the street corner consumed by our immediate material environment, we are under the influence of material consciousness. Our thoughts, feelings, beliefs, and sense of self are determined by the outer environment. Our intuitive and empathic awareness is focused on the energy of what is happening around us and the energies of those in our immediate environment.

Now imagine hiking up a lush green mountain. The rich scent of pine trees and the song of birds fill the air. After a while we come to a clearing where we are able to see how high we have climbed. There is a brook in the distance winding down the side of the mountain and flowing into a deep blue lake. Our heart and mind are clear and we feel a deep sense of peace. The beauty of our surroundings is inspiring. The worries and concerns that had been causing us stress seem to fall away.

We begin to wonder how we can rearrange our life to live full-time in this wonderful place we have discovered. We realize that it's going to take some work to make this happen. We have to sell our current home and figure out a way to get our employer to let us work remotely. As we think of the steps involved, we become less enchanted with the idea of moving. We wonder if it's even possible and become a bit discouraged. Still, we are determined to remain positive and try to make it happen.

As we come to rest along the mountain path, we perceive reality through mental consciousness. The beauty of our surroundings and the comfort and support we feel are symbolic of our increasing awareness of the love and support of spiritual presence. However, it takes effort on our part to make our dream of living in this energy and awareness a reality. With a lot to figure out, we get to work and forget the calm serenity of just being.

Now imagine being at the top of a mountain with a panoramic view of distant peaks. The sky is clear and the sun is shining down upon us. As we breathe, we can feel the pureness of the air moving through our being. As we contemplate the flight of a bird in the distance, we begin to merge with it and sail into the currents of the wind. In our heart, we feel a connection and oneness with this wise and loving creation. As a ray of sunshine streams into our vision, we dissolve into the warmth. Like laughter and smiles, the sunlight dances in the sky, brilliant and alive. We are the sunlight and the blue sky, the mountaintop, and more. We transcend physical form and feel ourselves as energy, immersed and supported by the force of love.

Atop the mountain's summit, we transcend the limitations of the physical realm. This is spiritual consciousness. We surrender to the flow of divine presence and allow ourselves to be fully supported. We experience a oneness with all of life and recognize the brilliant creative activity of a higher order that is always flowing with abundance. Our day-to-day needs and wants are met and manifest without worry, strife, or stress. We are not separate or apart from all of creation.

How to Scale the Heights

Given the beauty and bliss of the mountain, we may wonder why the person on the crowded and stinky streets doesn't just put on their hiking boots and scale the heights. That's a fair and logical question, yet there are many reasons that we may resist the calling of the bounty of higher vibrations.

Perhaps we have no interest in pursuing a higher consciousness. We like and feel comfortable in the city. We want the security of our friends, family, and the familiar. We have never climbed a mountain before and are a bit fearful and don't think we can make it. It may not make practical sense and seem too risky. Venturing into the unknown isn't appealing to us.

Maybe we very much want to live on the mountain, but we just can't figure how to make it work. We may come up with many reasons why it isn't possible. We are concerned about losing our job and making a career change. There are bills to pay and day-to-day responsibilities to take care of, and we may feel overly committed and have other responsibilities that we don't feel we can walk away from. We are concerned that we might be lonely and misunderstood by our friends and family. It just doesn't feel like the right time to make a drastic change. There are also unconscious reasons for not raising our level of consciousness, such as feeling unworthy, fearful, or stuck in the past.

When it comes to shifting our perspective about ourselves and our life into a higher awareness, there is often resistance. For those who are ready for this journey, the path is open. Once we set the intent to ascend into higher consciousness, there is a force within us and surrounding us that expertly weaves together the opportunities, synchronicities, and people who support this desire. We can take part in spiritual practices and exercises and do all the right things and still hold ourselves back. It is our intention and willingness that sets in motion the powerful current of consciousness transformation.

The spiritual challenge is to open to the vast panorama of who we are. Consciousness is fluid, and our awareness of ourselves, others, the world, and reality shifts and evolves. As empaths, intuitives, and sensitives, we are at an advantage. We are aware of and can often see, feel, sense, know, and accept the offerings of a broader energetic reality. Our challenge is to have courage and trust and release ourselves into the greater spiritual flow that is moving us forward into the flow of abundance, manifestation, and joy.

CHAPTER 5

Material Consciousness: External Power

For much of human existence, material consciousness has been the primary way through which we view ourselves and the world. It includes the belief that we must compete with one another and outer forces for survival. Through material consciousness, we define ourselves and the world around us through physicality, the five senses, and accepted cultural norms and beliefs. If we can touch, smell, hear, see, or taste something, it is real.

Through material consciousness, we are held in the grasp of cause and effect, finite time and space, and duality. No matter how hard we try, possibilities are limited. Material consciousness resides along the continuum of bad and good, right and wrong, success and failure, and joy and suffering. We experience both sides of duality. Some days we may be positive and feel like everything is going our way. We are making progress and creating the changes we wish to make. Then a short time later, we find ourselves confronting the same difficulties and challenges that we thought we had left behind.

Like the two sides of a coin, day and night, happiness and sadness, and gain and loss, we move back and forth along this never-ending continuum. Through material consciousness, change doesn't necessarily lead to transformation. Instead, it eventually leads us back to the same familiar problems. We begin to eat healthier, but if we are not vigilant, we slowly go back to our old eating habits. We find a new job to escape the drudgery of the old one, only to find ourselves in the same situation in the next job. One habit replaces another, and we continue to vacillate between what we want and what we don't want. Material consciousness keeps us struggling to achieve our desires, wants, and needs.

This material point of perception invites the belief that the universe turns a blind eye to us, that there is no power or influence that loves and cares for us unconditionally. It is only those who are strong, dominant, clever, or fortunate who thrive. For the most part, we still collectively approach many of our daily concerns through material consciousness. We fear lack, illness, poverty, and failure and believe that an unexpected calamity is never far away. Through material consciousness, such things as abundance, love, well-being, and inner peace don't come naturally or easily. We have to plot, plan, work hard, and be lucky in order to be successful and receive what we desire. The belief in struggle and opposition is so ingrained in material consciousness that it seems foolish to think otherwise.

Our ego does its best to think thoughts that provide us with a sense of power and control. The voice of the chattering mind supports reality as we have come to believe it to be. When we believe that external and random circumstances determine what opportunities and advantages come our way, our mind chatter will reinforce this belief. The chattering voice will continually remind us that we are no match for outer forces. We give away our power to others' opinions, the economy, and the cultural status quo. Focused on outer threats and material power, we cannot hear the quiet nuances of our heart and soul.

When we live primarily through material consciousness, life is often challenging, problematic, and difficult. Alternatively, it might also be sensuous and gratifying to the ego and satisfy our physical needs and desires. We often believe ourselves to be a victim of circumstances and try to control others and whatever comes our way to get what we desire. Harboring the secret fear that we are unworthy and vulnerable, we compare ourselves to others in order to feel more successful, dominant, and superior. The material perspective breeds competitiveness, struggle, selfishness, a fear of death, and a finite sense of what is possible. We have little self-awareness and a limited understanding of ourselves and life.

Through the perspective of material consciousness, we rely on ourselves and those we feel an affinity with to make our way through the world. Our identity is centered in physical characteristics such as our race and ancestry and our socioeconomic status. We adopt the beliefs and biases of our family and friends and don't veer far from the known and accepted. A successful life is based on external accomplishments and getting our needs and desires met. Through our personal effort, intelligence, family connections, education, talent, and some luck, we achieve. When something doesn't go the way we want it to, we blame ourselves, others, the economy, politics, or other outer forces. However, when things go as expected, we generally take full credit.

Material consciousness is connected primarily to the ego and our five senses. This orientation can satisfy us through a false sense of personal power and control and a materialistic drive. When our consciousness is centered in the material realm, we listen to the chattering voice. It makes sense to us, as its judgments and need for power and control reinforce the worldview of materiality.

Empathically Focused in the Material Realm

There are many intuitive, empathic, and sensitive people who perceive themselves and the world primarily through material consciousness. Most struggle to accept their intuitive insights, awareness of others' feelings, and extrasensory gifts. When our consciousness is focused in material reality, energetic, intuitive, and empathic sensations, feelings, and awareness are often ignored or doubted and dismissed. The voice in our head rebels against anything that it cannot fully grasp and understand. The chattering mind isn't able to fathom what is happening. The awareness that we are receiving and absorbing energy in the form of thoughts, feelings, and sensations doesn't make sense. When we believe only in what is physical and manifested, our reality becomes narrow and limited. The idea that unseen energy emits vibes that can influence and affect us doesn't fit into our belief in what is possible.

However, when our view is narrowly focused and we cease to explore the wonders of life and evolve, our soul continually nudges us into uncharted territory. One of the ways that it attempts to get our attention is through the emergence of intuitive and empathic awareness. Extrasensory experiences break through our rigid perceptions and open us to the nonphysical and unknown. Something within us awakens, and we begin to catch a glimpse of what lies beyond the purely material five senses.

However, material consciousness has a fickle relationship with the extrasensory realm. When our primary perception is based in material consciousness, we don't always accept the validity of intuitive and empathic sensitivity. Those who are open to the possibility that there is something beyond the physical reality that we can know, feel, and see generally feel that these abilities are possible only for some people, that extrasensory abilities are a special gift that lies beyond the scope of the average person's capabilities. However, even if we don't believe that intuitive and empathic sensing is real, we may still possess this ability.

When our primary view of reality is through material consciousness, intuitive and empathic energy is often experienced through the physical body. Vibes, gut feelings, and sensations such as shivers that run up and down the arms or the hairs on the back of the neck standing up are common. When we discount, fear, or deny the existence of the invisible realm of spirit and energy, we have no framework through which to receive intuitive guidance and insights. Extrasensory and nonphysical phenomena often invoke stress and anxiety. Our capacity to fully understand how we can intuit the feelings and vibes of others is limited.

Through material consciousness, the ego is the primary center of personal power. Because the ego likes to be dominant, extrasensory awareness is seldom trusted. Fear of the unknown has a long arm that extends into the empathic and intuitive realm. Unexpected intuitive awareness can be confusing or make us feel uneasy. We might not know what to do with intuitive information. We may not understand why we know and feel these things and what to do with what we receive. There may be no one we can turn to for advice, as we don't feel we can tell others what we are experiencing. Many people shut down and don't share their experiences with others for fear that they will be judged and seen as crazy or delusional. We might feel alone, odd, and different.

Despite the resistance and suspicion that those whose perception is based in material consciousness harbor toward extrasensory awareness, our empathic and intuitive sensitivity continues to get our attention. We may investigate and practice ways to psychically protect ourselves and avoid people and situations that feel threatening. We might also attempt to shut down our intuitive sensors and not feel.

Another challenge is ego interference. Once we embrace our intuitive inclinations, we are prone to allow our ego to interpret what we receive. When the ego gets involved, the chattering voice tells us the meaning of the intuited feelings, sensations, and insights we receive. Even though the ego isn't capable of connecting with energy information and correctly identifying its significance, this doesn't stop it from leading us, usually in the wrong direction.

The ego usually spins things in our favor and toward what we desire or it inspires fear and worry. The ego can lead us to believe that we are more talented, special, and gifted than others. We may tell ourselves that we have been graced with cosmic powers that demonstrate our superiority. If anyone questions us, we may attribute their attitude to jealousy, negativity, or our misunderstood brilliance. If we believe that we are infallible and more worthy than others, then we are more likely to manipulate others and use our gifts to gain attention and increase our sense of power.

Through material consciousness, we are vigilant when it comes to our survival and personal safety. The possibility that we might absorb the negative and potentially toxic and unhealthy energy of others is a concern. Because we are uneasy about the potential harmful effects of another's energy, we may avoid others and be careful about who we spend time with. The portrayal of the spiritual realm in popular culture as dark, evil, and dangerous has led many to avoid any interaction or connection with the unseen. Through material consciousness, we tend to be less aware of nuances and subtleties. We view the world in a more black-and-white, good-or-bad, "you're either with me or against me" kind of way. We trust the material world and our five senses.

Through material consciousness, the current of energy that we empathically and intuitively receive is focused primarily in the mundane world around us. This includes those we encounter on a day-to-day basis, our friends, family members, colleagues at work, and the energy of the environments we frequent. Because the material realm is ruled by duality, what we feel and intuit lies along the vast continuum of the positive and negative. While we may receive helpful and loving vibes and insights, we might also pick up on and absorb lower vibrations of negativity.

We may have a wide range of intuitive and extrasensory experiences, some more intense than others. We may begin to sense unknown influences that feel confusing or dark. Then unexpectedly, we experience what feels like a comforting presence or insights that are helpful to others. We might feel we are not alone, have strange dreams, or become increasingly fearful that there is something unseen that might cause us harm. Then seemingly out of nowhere, we feel the gentle warmth of a higher presence move through us and our heart opens.

···

EXERCISE
Inner Power

Through material consciousness, our initial response to problems, challenges, lack, and feeling limited is to look outside of ourselves for solutions. We might blame the economy, others, unforeseen circumstances, or bad luck for what we are experiencing. This often creates frustration, anger, and a sense of powerlessness.

When you feel overwhelmed by problems or challenges and begin to look outside of yourself for a solution, take a moment to breathe. There is a more effective way to proceed: go within and observe your feelings and thoughts.

What is the chattering voice telling you? Don't argue with it or try to convince yourself of what the inner voices are saying. Instead, just listen.

Breathe and release these feelings and thoughts through the exhale. Continue to breathe, and resist getting caught up in the chattering mind's inner dialogue. Breathe and exhale the stress and tension.

As you continue to breathe and let go of the thoughts and feelings through the exhale, remind yourself that you aren't your thoughts and feelings. Observe the voice of the chattering mind without attaching to its judgments, worries, and stress.

When the chattering mind begins to run out of steam, remind yourself that there is a greater source of presence and power within you.

Become aware of the center of power within your body. It may be in your solar plexus, your gut, or your heart, or maybe a feeling of power circulates through your being. It may feel like a rush of warm energy, love, and compassion or a force that helps you to feel grounded. You might also feel your inner power as sensations of tingling energy or a feeling of lightness or expanded awareness.

Listen to your power and let it speak to you.

Take some time to observe and feel this power. What does it want you to know and feel?

As you align with and listen to your inner power, you become aware of solutions, ideas, choices, and insights that perhaps you've never considered before. When we are ready to acknowledge the power within, we begin our ascension into mental consciousness.

••

The spiritual challenge in material consciousness is to recognize that our distress, anxiety, and concerns are driven by the belief that we are alone and powerless in an unloving world. If we believe that we are at the whim of external forces and the power of the material world, we live in fear. Our powerlessness feels real, and we collect evidence to support this belief. However, that doesn't mean that it's true. Through mental consciousness, we shift into the awareness of our inner power.

CHAPTER 6

Mental Consciousness: The Power of Thought

We earthlings have been operating primarily through material consciousness for a long time. With some exceptions, the world has been inclined to cling to the perception that what defines success is such things as power over others, economic and financial achievement, and proving ourselves to be better and more worthy than others. Throughout time, there have been great thinkers, philosophers, and open-minded individuals who have used thought, ideas, and the intellect to introduce a new way of perceiving the world and our lives. We are now more collectively evolving and awakening to the power of the mind.

Through material consciousness, our view of the world is influenced by our primal instincts. We are concerned mainly with survival and supporting and strengthening the ego. Mind or mental consciousness moves us beyond the belief that the power to influence and create what we desire resides in the physical world alone. Instead, the focus shifts from a purely physical perspective to the higher awareness of how to create what we desire through the power of our mind.

While material consciousness looks primarily to the outer world to know the self, the awakening of mental consciousness draws us inward in reflection and thought. Through moments of insight, we begin to perceive how our thoughts and intent influence what we experience. Slowly it becomes more evident that there is creative power in what we think and in our beliefs. As we examine how our thoughts and ideas influence our choices, decisions, and actions, we cannot help but become more aware of the power of our mind. Instead of believing that cultural, economic, and worldly influences determine our fate, we generate ideas and put effort into creative problem-solving. We may study current trends, look at helpful data, and consult with others to gain new knowledge. We better understand how information is power, and we form relationships with others based on our ability to communicate and share common ideas, beliefs, and aspirations. Our thoughts, ideas, and intellect are put to work to help with our concerns and worries and to achieve our desires.

Instead of believing that the outer world controls our destiny, we awaken to the realization that we are the cause of both our own suffering and our own happiness. As we evolve into the finer nuances of mental consciousness, we begin to recognize that when we have positive thoughts, beliefs, and intent, we attract positive experiences. It becomes more evident that perpetual negative thinking brings more negativity and unsatisfying outcomes our way. As we become more aware that what we manifest is built upon the foundation of our thoughts, feelings, ideas, beliefs, and imagination, we have new tools with which to create. We are no longer confined to pursuing what we want solely through physical effort and a focus on the external world.

The practice of using the power of our mind to achieve success in business and athletics and to attract what we desire is becoming more accepted.

As an example, it is becoming more popular for health and business professionals and athletes and motivational speakers to use positive thoughts and visualization to transform and achieve their goals and aspirations.

Mindfulness meditation and other similar visualization and positive thought practices use the power of the mind to heal and restore the mind, body, and spirit. We learned how to soothe and relax our thinking brain in order to visualize and focus our thoughts on creating what we desire. No longer a victim of circumstances that we have no control over, we harness the power of our mind to consciously create. We become aware that our thoughts, ideas, emotions, and intent lead to the attainment of our desires. Reality becomes more pliable as we create change from within ourselves. We are free from having to tackle a world that seems to be stacked against us.

However, as enlightening as it can be to use positive thoughts and intent to manifest our desires, it is also the unconscious mind, past experiences, and emotional patterns that we have developed over time that create the experiences of our day-to-day life. The unconscious mind is a potent force that we draw from on a daily basis, usually without knowing that we are doing so. It is the unknown within us that is often the architect of the situations and experiences that bring us pain and confusion. Until we become aware of the repressed and stuffed-away memories, beliefs, thoughts, and emotions within, we continue to sabotage and limit our ability to create what we desire.

Once we recognize the power of our thoughts, beliefs, and emotions, we are motivated to let go of sabotaging patterns, old wounds, and negative emotions. If we have thought of ourselves as a victim or as powerless, it can be startling when we realize that it is our beliefs and thoughts that are influencing and creating what we experience. This inspires many to become aware of and heal the unconscious mind and the beliefs and unhealed emotions that bring unsatisfying conditions.

Mental consciousness requires a consistent level of clear, positive thoughts and emotions and a healthy and healed unconscious mind to create and maintain our desired reality. When we slip into negative or self-defeating thoughts or feel disempowering emotions, the conditions that we would like to eradicate have the potential to quickly manifest.

For instance, we may want to increase our financial abundance or find a job that is more fulfilling, yet if we harbor the unconscious belief that we are unworthy and have little to contribute, this belief will limit our ability to attract money and meaningful work. No matter how much we use positive thoughts and affirmations, what we desire will not manifest. We will find ourselves continuing to experience the limitations that we have been trying to escape.

Another common error that occurs with mental consciousness is the tendency to allow our ego to dictate what will make us happy. As well-intentioned as our desires may be, we must be mindful of our motives. Without realizing it, our desires are usually generated from our ego. Although we may initially enjoy and successfully create and experience our longed-for outcomes, we might find that they provide only temporary satisfaction. Eventually we may not appreciate what we have and continue to pursue things that aren't aligned with our highest good. Continual striving and searching outside of ourselves for our happiness and joy leads to an inner emptiness. At some point, we discover that something is missing.

For instance, most of us desire to have more money, be in a loving relationship, have a comfortable home, and enjoy purposeful work. All of these desires and wants are acceptable to both our ego and our soul, as they provide us with an abundant and meaningful life. However, our ego's idea of abundance, the perfect partner, and a beautiful home may differ from our soul's needs and direction.

As an example, when our ego self makes a list of the desirable qualities of the type of person we would like as a partner, it might include such things as their occupation, income, physical characteristics, and shared and similar interests. Yet our soul is more interested in opportunities that expand our ability to love and receive love. It often directs us toward someone who can help us grow and heal deep wounds and inspire us to be our best.

Through mental consciousness, the chattering voice of our ego often directs our efforts toward what it deems to be important. For this reason, we may attract people, things, and conditions that are not as satisfying as what we had hoped for. We might manifest a relationship with someone who appears to have the qualities we desire, yet the relationship doesn't bring us the happiness and love we were seeking. We are not always as good at determining what will bring us joy as we think we are.

Intuitive and Empathic Mind

Through mental or mind consciousness, the existence of something beyond the physical realm becomes more compelling and accessible. We are more accepting of intuitive and empathic awareness and listen inward for helpful guidance and insights.

With new awareness of the inner and outer forces that might be hampering or blocking our desired outcomes, intuitive awareness becomes a valuable tool.

Through mental consciousness, the usefulness and benefits of our intuitive and empathic sensitivity become more clear. We begin to perceive it as an asset through which we can become more self-aware, better understand others, and create more of what we desire. Along with using our thoughts and feelings to create what we desire, we discover that our empathic and intuitive sensitivity can also assist us in experiencing more happiness and satisfaction.

For instance, let's say you are unsure of the right choice to make with an impending decision at work. After looking at all of the facts and data, you still feel that you don't have enough information. Instead of pushing yourself to figure it out, you take a step back and breathe and become centered. After clearing your mind, you ask within for guidance. Within a minute or two, you receive an insight about how the different options will affect your future with the company. In your heart and gut, you realize what the best choice is. In time, this proves to be correct.

As another example, perhaps a friend wants to set you up on a date with her boyfriend's friend. When she tells you the man's name, something feels off about him, but you agree to meet him anyway. A few days later, while sharing conversation and coffee with this man, the feeling that something isn't right intensifies. Although he is good-looking, confident, and easy to talk to, you decide not to see him again. A few months later, the friend who set you up informs you that the man you felt uneasy with was recently fired. He had been embezzling money for months, and the company is pressing charges against him.

Through mental consciousness, these kinds of experiences often persuade us to place more value on our intuition and empathy. Even though we may be uncomfortable with our energy sensitivity and abilities, we become more willing to explore the contribution that intuition can make to creating and manifesting our desires.

While mental consciousness opens us to the benefits of altered states of awareness and intuitive and empathic abilities, it is firmly centered in logic and reason. It was through the collective shift into mental consciousness that we as a people developed and embraced science. In time, many have come to believe that something is true and real only if there is evidence and physical proof. This creates a dilemma when it comes to trusting intuitive and empathic knowing. Scientific evidence of intuition's validity and reliability is scarce. While there have been many studies and psychic tests performed to authenticate or refute its validity, the results are often not taken seriously by the larger scientific community. Intuitive and empathic experiences defy the constraints of traditional science. If there is no scientific evidence to support the reliability of intuition and no proof that it is a viable means through which we can receive information, it is discounted. It might be a good theory or an interesting experience, but it doesn't hold weight or real value. As of yet, we have not developed the physical means through which we can measure and better understand nonphysical reality.

Mental consciousness can bring a level of chaos and stress to empathic and intuitive receptivity. The chattering voice that creates doubt and denies our intuitive and empathic awareness gets its strength from mental consciousness. While we may be more open to extrasensory experiences, there is a tendency to overthink and try to objectively dissect what we receive until it ceases to exist. Intuitive and empathic insights, feeling, knowing, sensations, and other phenomena are made up of vibrations and frequencies of energy. Intuitive energy cannot be accessed through the five senses or material methods or processes. We connect with intuitive energy through its vibration and frequency, and our brain interprets this energy and gives it meaning. However, when we overuse logic and reason to prove that intuitive and empathic sensitivity is real and valid, we lower our vibration and frequency. We can no longer rise to the higher frequency needed to receive energy information. The gift of the intuitive and empath is the ability to raise our vibration and energy frequency to the level of nonphysical energy and bring it into conscious awareness. However, the chattering mind interrupts and lowers our energy vibration, thereby instilling doubt and confusion.

The energy vibration and frequency of mental consciousness exists along a vast continuum. It has the potential to reach higher frequencies and access pure sources of energy information. However, overthinking and interference from the chattering voice often prevent intuitive receptivity and clarity. Mental consciousness resides within the duality of opposing forces, and we continually experience the positive and negative, the good and bad, happiness and sorrow. The energy that we intuit from others and our surroundings is also a mixture of varying emotions, feelings, and states of being.

The shift into understanding ourselves and the environment through mental consciousness can be a slow process. While some have evolved into this perception, many have not. We are still collectively awakening to the power that our thoughts, emotions, and subconscious have in creating our reality. Some people are introduced to mental consciousness through the spontaneous emergence of extrasensory awareness. Feeling the presence of spirit beings, experiencing synchronicities, sensing a guiding inner force, or knowing something without knowing how we know it can awaken us to our multidimensional nature.

The transition into mental consciousness helps us advance beyond a purely material sense of ourselves and reality. It has opened the door to the exploration of our potential and the possibilities that lie beyond the physical realm. This leads us into the expansive awareness of spiritual consciousness.

....

EXERCISE
Creative Manifestation

Through mental consciousness, we create and manifest through the power of the mind. This exercise will empower you to put your thoughts, imagination, and positivity to work. It utilizes visualization and an affirmation.

Think of a desire, need, or want that you would like to manifest. Form an image in your mind of what you would like to manifest and experience. Imagine it in as much detail as possible. Brighten up this image with color, texture, and vibrancy. Allow this image to come alive with emotion. Feel the happiness that comes when you experience what you would like to manifest and experience. Stay with this positive emotional energy for as long as possible. As you continue to fully feel the positive feelings, repeat an affirmation such as this one:

I am manifesting and embracing the _____ (relationship, job, increase in finances, etc.) that is quickly and easily coming into my life.

Become aware of any doubts or criticisms that surface. Don't try to push them away or ignore them. Allow them to surface.

If the chattering mind intrudes, breathe, relax, and thank it for its opinion. Don't attach to the doubts that surface. Breathe and let them go.

Create an image of yourself enjoying the manifestation of your desire, want, or need. See it in as much detail as possible, and express gratitude.

Throughout the coming days, weeks, or even months, continue to create an image of what you desire and repeat the affirmation.

The spiritual challenge of mental consciousness is to further explore the power of our thoughts and ideas. Our thoughts are powerful, and they materialize and manifest as the circumstances, opportunities, people, and abundance that we experience daily. Becoming aware of the power of the mind enables us to better understand how energy is the building block of manifestation.

Once we recognize that we can manifest through allowing and surrendering to a higher force and power, we begin to transform. It may be a challenge to let go of our ego's need to control everything. However, as our relationship with energy and the unseen expands and deepens, we evolve into spiritual consciousness.

CHAPTER 7

Spiritual Consciousness: The Force of Love

The most significant impact that we can have on our life and the lives of others and the planet is the transformation of material and mental consciousness into spiritual consciousness. However, we don't always have a clear understanding of what it means to be spiritual.

For some, being spiritual involves practicing such things as meditation, mindfulness, or yoga and embracing a collection of principles and beliefs. For others, it is the ability to sense a higher divine presence and practice love, compassion, kindness, and forgiveness toward ourself and others. The awakening of our true and eternal nature as spirit and soul and the transcendent awareness of being connected to the oneness of all of life define spirituality for many. Those who have the ability to sense energy and spirits, angels, and higher divine beings often describe themselves as spiritual. There isn't just one definition of spirituality, as it is a personal and individual experience.

Although many of the beliefs and practices of spirituality are integrated within spiritual consciousness, they aren't the same.

Spirituality encompasses the vast and individual exploration of such things as a greater power or being, the understanding that our life has purpose and meaning, and practices to deepen self-awareness and extrasensory experiences. In contrast, spiritual consciousness is the communion and the merging of higher frequencies of divine presence and activity within our mind, body, and spirit. It isn't an orientation or a set of practices, beliefs, and exercises. While these things can support our ascension, spiritual consciousness transcends linear and rational thought and understanding.

Material consciousness is centered in the concrete, physical realm, and mental consciousness is centered in our mind and thoughts. Through spiritual consciousness, our awareness is centered in spirit and soul and differs from material and mind consciousness in fundamental ways. Through material and mental consciousness, the focus is on utilizing our personal power to create success and happiness. Spiritual consciousness doesn't rely on our personal efforts alone. Instead, it is the allowing of a divine creative force to flow into our lives and manifest as our highest good.

Through material consciousness, we trust our ego and physical power and abilities to guide us. Power is found in such things as brute strength, outer achievements, force, and an abundance of money and connections with influential people. When our awareness is centered in mental consciousness, our power center is our mind and thoughts. Through spiritual consciousness, power has new meaning. Instead of relying on worldly power and our ability to manifest what we desire through positive thinking, we allow our good to flow to us. We are no longer at the whim of random and outer forces that have the ability to bring us joy or misery. Spiritual consciousness is the awareness that there exists only one power and it can never oppose itself. It is always in alignment with our highest good.

How we define and understand the divine creative force varies from individual to individual. For some it is simply a higher power, while for others it is God, Spirit, truth, or nature. I have come to view this as divine presence and the force of love—not our human interpretation of love, but the divine and holy presence of love as the foundation through which all of creation is born, nourished, and sustained. It is through opening our heart to the force of love that the divine presence becomes the creative activity of our consciousness. As we absorb and allow this high-vibration energy to flow through our being, it manifests through such things as abundance in all forms, relief from suffering, solutions in the midst of obstacles, and mental, emotional, and physical healing.

Beyond Duality

Through material and mental consciousness, we are under the dictates of duality. In between the forces of good and bad and positive and negative, there lies a vast continuum. Our emotions, thoughts, and experiences travel along this never-ending path of all possibilities. We experience varying degrees of the good and the not-so-good. Such things as loss and gain, health and illness, success and failure, happiness and depression, and hope and fear follow us throughout our days.

Mental consciousness attempts to move us into the higher vibrations of the good. Through positive thinking and affirming our desires, the power of the mind is employed to ensure we experience more of what we desire. However, we must continually monitor our thoughts and emotions to keep focused on the positive. Still, despite our constant effort, vigilance, and focus, contradictory influences are always present. The bad follows the good, things fall apart after being put back together, and we experience varying degrees of the positive and negative. Internal and external forces are always present that appear to oppose each other.

Spiritual consciousness offers us freedom from duality and the continuous cycle of conflicting forces. Opposing states such as good and evil, lack and abundance, and suffering and relief don't exist in the higher frequencies of the divine. When divine creative activity is at work within our consciousness, it can manifest only as the good. We still live in the physical world of duality, but it doesn't have a hold on us. Our being vibrates within the harmony of the one power that is not limited by material laws.

In this world we will always encounter a variety of experiences, feel a wide range of emotions, and think an array of thoughts. This is the reality of the material world. Spiritual consciousness doesn't keep us from experiencing the full range of being human. Instead, it opens us to a higher dimension of reality. It doesn't change us so much as transport us into a part of ourselves where the pure source of goodness and love flows endlessly. It is in these higher aspects of the self that the divine resides.

For instance, imagine that when you get out of bed in the morning you feel a variety of aches and pains. Your neck is tight, your head hurts, and your body feels heavy and sore. A short time later you sit outdoors on your patio next to a flower-filled garden and watch the sun come up. The birds are singing and you experience a deep sense of peace and communion with all that surrounds you. You are not aware of your aches and pains and stiffness anymore. Instead, your awareness is focused on the harmony of your surroundings, and you feel only peace and connectedness with the beauty you are immersed in.

Through spiritual consciousness, our day-to-day lives aren't determined and controlled by random and external conditions and the chattering voice of the ego. We no longer feel a compelling duty to control, change, and improve ourselves and our circumstances in order to be happy. As we take in and absorb the force of love, it becomes our experience. There is no need to search outside of ourselves for answers or to worry about how to get our needs met. Instead of trying to move mountains and attain what we desire solely through our physical and mental efforts, we allow a greater spiritual force to create and manifest our higher good through us. While the material world will always give us contrast and duality, our awareness centered in the power and force of love lifts us out of its grasp.

Duality and finite limitations will always be a part of the physical world we live in. However, when we vibrate to spiritual consciousness, outer circumstances don't define what we experience. Through logic and rational thought, this makes no sense. If the conditions we find ourselves in are not to our liking, we are generally unhappy and dissatisfied. However, in the midst of circumstances that have the appearance of discord and misfortune, spiritual understanding and peace sustain us.

Spiritual consciousness can never be fully defined and understood through material and mental consciousness, as it defies reason and the limitations of the physical and material laws. As divine presence becomes the activity of our consciousness, we don't blame outer conditions or our thoughts for what we experience. Instead, we come to the realization that everything we encounter is essential to our soul's journey. We know that we are more than our physical body and that our soul incarnates in the physical realm to further our evolution. There is purpose and meaning to our challenges and the conditions we face on a daily basis. The thinking brain isn't able to provide us with this essential understanding. Until we accept that everything can be used by the divine presence for our highest good, our troubles continue to follow us wherever we go.

When we open our heart and listen within, the divine interpretation of our problems and difficulties is revealed. Through revelations and insights into the higher truths embedded in our challenges, we integrate the higher states of spiritual consciousness into our everyday lives. This transference of high-frequency energy creates inner harmony and manifests in such things as the working out of our concerns, abundance of all kinds, a renewed sense of purpose, and positive opportunities.

Spiritual Intuition

Spiritual consciousness embraces conscious communion with spiritual forces. We can best become aware of the force of love in quiet moments of inner listening and sensing. Empathic and intuitive awareness is the channel through which we can receive these higher vibrations. Although our extrasensory awareness tends to absorb and pick up on the energy of others and the external world, its divine function is to connect us with the higher vibrations of light.

We tend to believe that intuitive and empathic sensing is focused primarily in the things of the material realm. Through material and mental consciousness, our intuitive and empathic awareness can feel like a jumble of feelings, images, sensations, and knowing that don't always make sense. We would like our extrasensory abilities to help us improve our day-to-day lives, solve our problems, and increase our abundance. However, when we try to control it, we soon discover that it is not always as effective as we would like it to be. As much as we would like to use our intuitive and empathic awareness in specific ways, it often has its own agenda. While we may receive comforting and guiding insights and messages, some sensations, feelings, and impressions are confusing or feel negative. While we may empathically know how another feels and be able to tune into their moods and even their thoughts, we might not know what to do with the awareness that we receive.

It may seem inconceivable that our intuitive and empathic channels can be the source through which higher forces flow into our lives and manifest as our highest good, yet intuitive and empathic awareness plays an essential role in shifting us into spiritual consciousness. When we focus our intuitive and empathic awareness within and observe and listen without attaching to what moves through us, the noise of the outer world begins to subside. Underneath the ego thoughts and our worries, concerns, and stress, spiritual forces are present. In the stillness and quiet of our heart, an elusive yet intimate presence begins to peek through. An inner whisper of love and wisdom calls out to us. While the chattering voice does all it can to dismiss the gentle rippling of the divine incoming tide, the force of love breaks through and opens us to the awareness of higher forces.

Through spiritual consciousness, our extrasensory awareness expands beyond the confines of the material realm. As the grip of the material realm loosens, a higher love enters our being. Inner divine presence becomes more tangible and real. We don't have to be good or perfect humans to attain spiritual consciousness.

Like drops of rain that create a stream which eventually makes its way to the sea, the force of love becomes the activity within our consciousness, little by little. With each touch of spiritual presence, we transform. New perceptions and insights flow into our being, mind, and heart.

As we become still, listen within, and allow the force of love to flow into our being, we pay attention to signs of this heightened shift. We may experience it as a tingling tremor, a feeling of expansion in our head or mind, or a soothing ripple of love or a warmth in our heart. The high vibrations of divine presence may feel like inner shivers of electricity, a murmur of energy moving through our body, or soft and warm sensations running down our spine. In this transcendent awareness, our inner being smiles and relaxes.

The divine force of love may speak to us through quiet whispers and seek to get our attention in countless ways. It might be through an inner knowing that all is well when we are stressed or worried or a feeling of comfort after a loss. Sometimes a warm, gentle wave of assurance that we are cared for and that our lives have purpose and meaning moves into our being. While in the depths of despair or depression, we may feel a presence reaching out, offering solace, healing, and renewal. In moments of realization, we feel and know the divine purpose and meaning inherent in our day-to-day challenges and receive enlightened guidance and synchronicities. Through inner guidance, we receive enlightened messages that direct us to the people, situations, and choices that are in our highest good. Although these feelings and insights can be quiet and subtle, there is an inner assurance that accompanies them.

Our sensitivity and empathic and intuitive abilities no longer feel overwhelming, confusing, or negative. Instead, a spaciousness and the expansion of spiritual consciousness moves us beyond a finite ego-based framework. As the breath of the divine flows into our being from our intuitive and empathic senses, a deep alchemy takes place. No longer tethered to the material laws, the infusion of higher-frequency divine energy expresses itself as all forms of abundance, including such things as an increase in finances, career opportunities, solutions to problems, physical healing, and harmony in our relationships. While the challenges, difficulties, and issues that are inherent in the physical world may still arise, a way is made.

The transition into the lofty heights of spiritual consciousness happens gradually and in moments of connection with the divine. This is more than a thought or an awareness. It is the inner transformative process from ego-centered awareness to the alignment of our mind, body, and spirit with the force of love. As we surrender our direction and our problems, desires, worries, and stress to divine presence, we enter into the realm of all creative possibilities.

The shift into complete spiritual consciousness is rare in this world. There are extraordinary healers and great teachers such as Buddha, Jesus, and many saints from all spiritual traditions who have attained this full state of consciousness. There are also many unknown individuals who have entered into a profound state of illumination and grace through spiritual consciousness. However, even a moment spent in communion with the unyielding love and devotion of the force of love is transformative. Just a few minutes in communion with the divine presence as the activity within our consciousness has the power to manifest as the good in all areas of our lives.

....

MEDITATION
The Flow of Light

The force of love is light that knows no darkness and has no opposition. It is not influenced by the events of the world and cause and effect. It is always goodness and love, and it comes into physical form through the divine creative activity within our consciousness.

This meditation will help you invite higher-frequency divine energy into your being and become more familiar with these sensations and feelings as it moves through you. You may want to write down what you feel and receive and keep a journal of all of the meditations, practices, and exercises in this book.

To begin, take a long, deep breath and send the energy of the breath through you. Allow it to loosen and release any tension in the body. Release this tension through the exhale, let go, and relax. Continue to breathe in this gentle way as you release any stress, tension, and toxicity in the body.

As you breathe and relax, imagine the most powerful vibrational force that exists, stronger than the sun or gravity or the movement and power that set the stars in place and the planets and the universe in motion. This force is love, and it heals, nurtures, supports, and manifests all things. It flows through every living being in physical form and in the formless.

Take a long, deep breath and imagine the force of love as vibrant light flowing into your being and merging with your breath. As you breathe and invite the light of the force of love to flow through you, it becomes your breath and surrounds you.

As you breathe and relax, continue to imagine the force of love as a white light pulsating and collecting a bit above your head. As you breathe and rest in this energy, you may feel, sense, and experience a heightened vibration or density and see images, light, or colors.

Breathe and imagine this white-light energy flowing down through the top of the head and moving through you. Feel the cells of your body strengthen and rise to a higher rate of vibration. You may experience the movement of the force of love through your being as shivers of energy, tingling sensations, a feeling of your spirit lifting beyond the physical body, and the feeling that your heart is expanding.

As you continue to breathe vibrant white light down through the top of your head, allow it to collect in your mind and feel a sense of expansion. This nurturing, cleansing, and sustaining energy is both invigorating and calming at the same time. You may sense this presence or see or feel spots of white and purple energy.

Inhale and feel the flow of the force of love as a ring of blue energy surrounding your throat and upper shoulders. Relax your jaw and breathe, exhaling any tension. Continue to breathe and then say aloud or within, "I am." Exhale and feel the rise in your vibration. On the inhale, continue to repeat the phrase "I am." Breathe and rest in the divine presence, and allow the force of love to move through your inner being.

As you continue to breathe, the energy of the force of love collects in your heart. Your heart fully opens to this light as shades of green, turquoise, and white-light energy move through you. Feel the higher frequency of the force of love expand within your heart. As you continue to breathe, love and compassion flow into any emotional wounds, resentments, pain, or grief stored in your heart. Allow any feelings to surface. If your heart feels tight or restricted, continue to inhale and invite the force of love to move through you. Exhale and let go of whatever no longer serves you.

As the force of love continues to flow through your breath, allow it to move into your solar plexus, filling you with white light. Continue to breathe, and imagine a spiral of orange energy surrounding you. Breathe into your center of power and intuition, your solar plexus. Feel this power as the expansion of consciousness and awareness.

Continue to breathe the light of the force of love down through the top of the head and move it down just a bit below your belly button. As this energy builds up, soak it in and allow it to nurture and support the attainment of your highest potential and happiness in this life. Imagine the force of love flowing into every area of your life. Your relationships, career, health, finances, and life path rise into the higher vibrations of manifestation. The force of love manifests as goodness in perfect form.

Like a luminescent waterfall, the white light of the force of love flows from above your head to the soles of your feet, bathing you in higher-frequency energy. As this light moves through your body, allow it to cleanse and clear you of any limited thoughts and emotions that keep you from being a clear channel of light.

Rest in the quiet inner silence and listen. Open your heart and become aware of any messages, insights, visions, and sensations. Observe without grasping or engaging the mind.

···

Empaths, intuitives, and sensitives are often more aware of the depth of love that the invisible realm has for us. We embody the sublime inner senses that allow us to more easily feel and sense the presence of higher-vibration love. Comfortable on the border of the physical and nonphysical, we move into and out of the sublime and the manifest. We are better able to decipher the meaning and message within what is difficult to fully grasp through our five material senses alone.

As we invite the force of love into our being, our vibration shifts little by little, moment by moment. As divine activity becomes the creative force within our consciousness, our highest good flows into manifestation.

The spiritual challenge is to embrace the awareness that our intuitive and empathic sensitivity can serve as the channel through which we raise our level of consciousness and live a more abundant, joy-filled, and purposeful life.

By design and nature, we embody spiritual consciousness. There is nothing to get or to attain. It is more of a letting go of who we have thought ourselves to be and releasing the accumulation of stuffed emotions and old wounds, beliefs, and energy cords that block our light. Our work is to release all that crowds out our ability to ascend into the vibrations of light.

In the next section, we explore the process through which we raise our vibration so that we can merge and live within spiritual consciousness.

PART III
Letting Go

CHAPTER 8

How We Intuit, What We Intuit

We are all on a path of ascension into spiritual consciousness. Even when it seems that we are moving in the opposite direction, the divine is calling to us. However, we aren't always aware of its gentle whispers and guiding presence. This step of our journey into spiritual consciousness begins with refining our ability to feel and tune into the energetic subtleties within our mind, body, heart, and spirit. Increased energetic awareness empowers us to choose the energy frequency that we wish to intuit, absorb, and receive.

Consciousness isn't centered in a part of our body. It isn't derived from our brain, heart, or nervous system. The root of our awareness and consciousness is in our spirit. The same can be said of intuitive and empathic awareness. It is a function of our nonphysical self. Although consciousness and extrasensory awareness are expressed through our physical self, this awareness isn't contained within our body. The roots of our consciousness and extrasensory awareness extend into our spirit. The common thread that winds through our empathic and intuitive awareness and consciousness is energy. The shift into higher awareness and becoming a channel for divine creative activity begins with refin-ing our ability to tune into energy and choose the frequency we wish to intuit and absorb.

Material consciousness is aligned with what is tangible and appeals to our five senses. Our awareness of energy is limited, and it isn't perceived as a significant factor in our overall well-being. Yet even though we may discount the role that energy plays in our daily lives, we are still subject to its influence. The subtle and physically undetectable energy that everything and everyone exudes impacts our well-being on many levels. When we cease to listen to our heart and spirit, we suffer. Without inspiration, a sense of purpose, and the higher vibrations of the force of love moving through us, we are more prone to such things as depres-sion, anxiety, worry, and ill health.

Our lack of awareness of the influence of energy can also lead us to trust others even when that little something inside of us tells us not to. For instance, Angie had a friend who was invest-ing money in a tech start-up. Angie's friend Henry assured her that if she invested soon, she was sure to make a lot of money. That night Angie had a hard time getting to sleep. She had an upset stomach and woke up from a dream that left her uneasy. The next day Henry called and told her that if she wanted to invest, she would have to do it soon. Remembering the previous night's dis-turbed sleep and stress-filled dream, she hesitated for a moment, then dismissed the idea that it was a warning or was related to the investment. Two and a half years after Angie invested a large sum in the business, it folded and her money was lost.

Those familiar with the dynamics of energy know that we can receive information and guidance from the sensations in our body and through our dreams. Even though we may not be consciously aware of all of the facts of a situation, energy doesn't lie.

Through mental consciousness, we have a better grasp of the importance of energy. We understand that it is the energy of our thoughts, beliefs, and emotions that creates and manifests what we experience. We are more aware of the influence of energy and work to control and manage our thoughts and feelings. However, while we may feel the energy of positive thoughts and emotions, we are still prone to being overly influenced by our ego and the chattering voice.

Through doubt and fear, the chattering mind discourages us from listening to and trusting what we intuitively feel and know in our heart and spirit. It confuses us with its insistence that our ego is the ultimate judge of reality. Far too often, we listen to the familiar and insistent chattering mind and remain captive to the illusions. It is easy to get locked into a mindset of struggle and continue to listen to the constant voices in our head that drown out the whispers of the quiet inner presence. When we allow our ego to determine our course, we are held in its tight grip. For the most part, we trust its more analytical thought process, which keeps us focused on the difficulties of everyday life and in fear of what might happen.

When we make choices and decisions primarily through the logical thinking mind, we often find ourselves out of sync with our greater good and in soul-deadening relationships and situations.

As an example, a job that may not logically appear to be a good fit or provide us with what we think we want and need may have hidden potential for positive and fulfilling outcomes.

We may ignore a synchronistic chance meeting with someone because their appearance doesn't fit our ideal of a desirable mate.

When we don't listen within to the whispers of our heart, we misjudge the positive and fulfilling possibilities that come our way.

Spiritual consciousness is dynamically different. We embody a refined sensing of the subtleties of energy and better understand the importance of aligning with high-frequency energy. Our sense of soul, spirit, and essence cannot be fully understood through the logical thinking mind or the five senses. The journey into spiritual consciousness is a fundamental shift away from relying on the material realm's definition of reality. Instead, we invite a new vision and understanding of who we are and what is possible to emerge. This begins with listening within to our heart and the soft whispers of our inner voice.

One of the gifts that intuitive, sensitive, and empathetic awareness offers us is the ability to break through the illusory nature of the material world and perceive truth through a more expansive lens. It is through our heart and spirit and not our logical brain that we hear the whispers of truth. As we listen within and open ourselves more fully to the force of love, our intuitive sensing comes to life. Something intangible and nonphysical makes its way into our awareness, calling us into a deeper part of ourselves. When we listen within, we connect with our most powerful self.

Empaths and the intuitive and sensitive are inherently better able to feel, sense, know, and connect with the less tangible realm of energy and vibration. With a more refined ability to sense, feel, and connect with the nonphysical realm, we are well equipped to lead the shift into spiritual consciousness. It is through our spiritual senses that the power and potential of energy comes to life.

Being Energy

As we listen within and tune into the understated energies of our intuition, the gateway into spiritual consciousness opens. While we may appear to be purely physical beings, our true nature extends far beyond our physicality. The analytical mind can have some difficulty conceptualizing ourselves as light, vibration, and subtle energy. Because we have come to know our material environment through our physical senses and our thinking brain, it's hard to imagine and comprehend that everything we encounter is vibrating energy. What appears to be solid and purely physical is slow, dense vibrating energy. Our thoughts and feelings are a less dense form of material vibration, and our soul and spirit an even lighter vibration.

In large part, our understanding of ourselves as energy is confined to the energy that our body needs to be healthy and active. We generate energy through the foods we eat and the amount of exercise and sleep we get. Even so, this is not a complete picture of our energy needs and sensitivities. While we know that our body converts food into energy, we are less aware of how the energy of our thoughts and emotions and higher sources of spiritual energy affect and influence us.

For instance, despite eating well and getting enough sleep and exercise, we may experience times when we have low energy and times when we feel fully alive and vibrant. This is often due to the energy of our emotions and thoughts. The kind words or touch of a new love can send tingles of energy through us and fill us with vitality. Feeling inspired, excited, and happy increases our energy, while disappointment and grief can make us feel tired and worn-out. When we experience a breakup or a loss, we may barely be able to get out of bed. Our mind may be foggy and we might lack the energy to get through the day. It's the same with our thoughts. When we think of a goal we achieved or an upcoming vacation we are looking forward to, we have more energy. If we continually think about a job interview that didn't go well or a past hurtful event, we are bound to feel down and depressed.

Every thought and feeling we experience carries an energetic charge. If we pay attention and tune into the energy of our emotions and thoughts, we discover that everything we experience has a vibe. These vibrations are like the notes of a musical scale. Emotions such as happiness and kindness have a high vibration, while depression and negativity have a lower vibration. Emotions like love and joy give us energy, while emotions and thoughts that are negative or filled with resentment or sadness are heavier. This low energy drains and tires us.

Our overall energy vibration influences our level of consciousness. In material consciousness, our vibes, often fueled by such things as fear and worry, are low and heavy. The vibes of mental consciousness are a bit higher and lighter. We are more aware of our inner power and ability to create, and this inspires more positive energy. Through spiritual consciousness, we receive the lofty vibrations of the force of love and rise into the frequency of divine presence.

However, we all continually feel both positive and negative emotions and all the feelings in between. No one emotion is more spiritual than any other emotion, and it is essential that we allow ourselves to feel what we genuinely feel. It is not the random negative thought or feeling of sadness or anger that lowers our energy vibration. Instead, it is our tendency to hold onto and repress difficult and painful emotions and unhealed wounds that lowers our vibration.

All too often, we don't allow ourselves to fully feel our feelings. This keeps the energy of our emotions stuck within our body and energy field. Emotions such as sadness, grief, and anger are uncomfortable and difficult to fully feel. Trauma, loss, pain, and hurt, especially the pain we experience in childhood, can feel impossible to bear. We may fear that we don't have the capacity to deal with the intensity of trauma and overwhelming feelings of grief.

When we suppress and stuff down our emotions and feelings, they become embedded in our body and energy field. This creates energy blocks and prevents the life-giving energy of the force of love from freely moving through us. Our stuffed-away and repressed difficult emotions and feelings keep us locked in habitual feelings of negativity, anger, and resentment. As much as we would like to forget, ignore, and leave behind past difficult and painful experiences, the unhealed energy remains within us. Unfortunately, we don't always know how to heal and let go of the past. Even if we have put past traumas and old wounds behind us, the unhealed energy doesn't just evaporate.

Even when we are no longer aware of them, our unhealed and repressed emotions influence and affect our emotional, mental, and physical health. Stored in our body, our unhealed emotional energy becomes a silent but powerful presence. Heart attacks, cancer, and problems with the digestive, nervous, and endocrine systems are often rooted in our unresolved past. Eating disorders, addictions, depression, abuse, unhappiness, and suicide can stem from unhealed and repressed emotions and trauma. Chronic emotional patterns of anger, rage, resentment, hopelessness, or a fear of abandonment signal the presence of unresolved and stuffed-away emotions and unhealed wounds and trauma.

Stuffed-away pain and unhealed wounds lower our vibration and keep us confined to a reality of suffering and struggle.

We Attract What We Repress

When we fully feel our emotions instead of stuffing them down and repressing them, they dissipate. No matter how uncomfortable and difficult our pain and suffering may be, feeling our emotions allows them to pass through us and be released. When we are overwhelmed by our emotions and repress, deny, or don't acknowledge them, they become detrimental. Stuffed-away emotions emit an energetic charge that attracts similar emotional energy.

The law of attraction is a universal phenomenon wherein like attract likes. The emotions that we repress or deny draw to us people and experiences that embody these same emotions. What we repress and stuff down into our body and energy field is a magnet that attracts similar energy.

For instance, if you grew up in a family that kept secrets or lied about important issues and you've stuffed down the hurt and confusion this caused, you will likely attract circumstances of betrayal and dishonesty. Even if you vow to choose friends and partners who are open and authentic, you may find yourself repeating the same pattern. You will also be sensitive and reactive to the slightest hint of dishonesty or betrayal from friends, family, coworkers, and others.

Our stuffed-away and repressed emotions also surface and increase the intensity of the pain and suffering we experience in similar current emotional experiences.

For instance, if a loved one passes away when we are young and we repress and stuff down the grief, we are likely to attract loss in some form. Our unfelt past emotions and grief are easily triggered. Just the thought of a friend or partner leaving a relationship can invoke fear and cause us profound stress. When someone does leave us, the pain is so much deeper because of the past hurts and traumas still embedded in our body.

The emotions and wounds we repress and trap in our physical body and energy field also influence and affect our perceptions and judgments. When the pain, discomfort, or negativity that we experience seems too much to bear, we may unknowingly stuff this energy down into the body and absorb it into our energy field that extends from the body.

How we view ourselves and others is tainted by this emotional energy and our thoughts and feelings. We don't perceive ourselves, others, and life as they are. We see it all through the lens of our energy patterns.

For instance, if your physical body and energy field is riddled with unhealed past wounds, stuffed-away difficult emotions, or negativity, you may perceive constant threats to your well-being and attract troublesome people and unfavorable experiences.

Overthinking and continually recalling the pain of a past trauma or hurt without resolving it can also lead to unhealthy emotional patterns.

For instance, perhaps a past family member or spouse treated you unfairly and took advantage of you. You go over and over what happened in your mind, each time becoming more upset and angry. Eventually the emotions connected to this experience act like a magnet, drawing people and experiences that sabotage your happiness and well-being.

Not only do our past stuffed-away emotions create energy patterns and inner blockages, but our thoughts and beliefs become ingrained in our energy field as well. Imagine that you have been told over and over since you were a child that life is full of struggle and it's hard to get ahead. These thoughts and beliefs form an energy pattern within your energy field. They act like an energetic net, attracting people, situations, and experiences that create struggles that keep you stuck.

Our Strongest Vibe

The energy that we consistently intuit, feel, and sense in others is similar to our strongest energetic vibe. As sensitives, empaths, and intuitives, we are especially likely to intuit the emotions and thoughts of those whose energy is similar to our own.

Have you ever wondered why, in a group of people, you intuit and sense the emotions and energy of a particular person? Let's say you are in a meeting or at a party and you begin to feel the vibes of someone in the room—not the vibes of everyone in the room, but just those of a specific person. When you pay attention to what you intuitively feel, absorb, and pick up, you might begin to notice that the feelings and thoughts you are receiving are familiar. You may have or have had friends or family who expressed these same feelings and thoughts or been in the company of others who did. However, it is even more likely that the energy you intuit from another is similar to your own repressed energy. As empaths, intuitives, and sensitives, we tend to more easily feel and intuit the thoughts and emotions of others that mirror our own thoughts and feelings. Vibes that feel familiar get our attention and are easier to intuit and sense.

As an example, perhaps you are attending a conference and you suddenly begin to feel anxious. This is surprising because just a few minutes earlier you felt relaxed. You begin to feel your throat tighten as your anxiety level rises. Feeling a bit of panic, you excuse yourself and go outside to get some fresh air. A few minutes later, you feel better.

As you walk back into the event, you notice a woman behind a podium speaking about her past trauma and anxiety. You realize that you were introduced to her right before you began to feel anxious. Although it may seem like a stretch from a logical point of view, you feel as if you intuitively absorbed her anxiety when you shook her hand. Although she didn't mention that she was one of the speakers during your short conversation or that she was anxious, you felt it. As you listen to her speak, you have empathy and compassion for her. You, too, are anxious about public speaking and appreciate her honesty in addressing it.

Here are some of the common energies that we intuit, absorb, and feel in others that may be a reflection of our unconscious and repressed energy:

- Emotional pain and suffering
- Grief, anger, fear, and resentment
- Negative or self-defeating thoughts and beliefs
- Physical illness, aches, and pains
- Emotional, physical, mental, and spiritual exhaustion
- Anxiety, stress, and panic

It's not just others' difficult and challenging emotions that pick up on and intuit; we might intuit and feel the light and positive feelings of others as well. Those who radiate optimism and help us to feel happy can raise our energy vibration without saying a word. While we may feel tired, sad, or hopeless in the company of someone who has a more negative perspective, those who radiate love often uplift and energize us. In any given social or work situation, we find ourselves in the company of people of different levels of consciousness and vibration. We naturally gravitate toward and intuitively feel more comfortable with others who have a similar vibe as ours. Once we release and let go of repressed emotions and heal old wounds, we attract lighter, more positive energy. Wherever we go, we absorb the good vibrations and radiate this energy out to others.

Here are some common higher-frequency energies that we may intuit, sense, and feel in others:

- Inspiration
- Love
- Acceptance
- Authenticity
- Peace
- Relaxation
- Increase in physical energy
- Generosity

Just as we stuff down or deny our difficult emotions, we might also repress our soul's purpose and gifts. When we feel unworthy and not good enough to embrace and express our talents and abilities, we detach from them. We may fear that we might embarrass ourselves or fail to achieve what we know in our heart is right for us. If we have been chronically disappointed and let down throughout our life, we may not be able to take risks and believe in ourselves. When we are enmeshed in material consciousness, we don't always trust our soul longings and may believe our dreams and aspirations are impractical and unrealistic.

When we have repressed our natural abilities and soul gifts, they lie dormant within us. The people we admire and the talents of others that we enjoy and envy can provide insight into our own gifts.

Practice acknowledging and opening your heart and mind to the traits, talents, and abilities that you admire in others. Imagine participating in similar activities and let your imagination run wild. When you align with the good in others, you gain confidence in expressing and embracing aspects of yourself that you may have been ignoring.

Sensing, feeling, and absorbing the energy of others as they express their gifts allows us to *try on* these energies. We can get a feel for what it is like to have musical talent, develop our psychic abilities, practice healing, or be a leader. However, if we don't recognize that these same gifts are alive within us, we miss the opportunity to further develop and express them.

Here are some common gifts and abilities that may lie dormant within us:

- Speaker, leader, healer
- Inventor, innovator, entrepreneur
- Musician, singer, actor
- Writer, athlete, chef
- Artist, creative talent
- Intuitive, medium, and psychic abilities

Feeling, sensing, and intuiting another's kindness and compassion and loving heart can tell us a lot about our ability to love. Opening our heart and absorbing the loving energy of another increases our capacity to love and heal others. Here are a few qualities we might notice in others that we likely have within ourselves:

- Strength
- Courage

- Leadership
- Compassion
- Kindness
- Unconditional love
- Joy

How Consciousness Influences What We Intuit

Our level of consciousness and the emotions, thoughts, and energy that we absorb and intuit go hand in hand. The energetic frequency of what we absorb and intuit influences our level of consciousness, while in turn, our level of consciousness influences the vibes that we absorb and intuit. They are inextricably intertwined.

Material Consciousness

For those who are centered primarily in material consciousness, feelings aren't ethereal and lofty. They are down-to-earth and span the wide range of emotional possibilities. Through material consciousness, emotions spur us to action and help us make choices and decisions. Instead of feeling our emotions, we tend to act on them.

For instance, through material consciousness, we are likely to experience love as romance and devotion to family and friends. We may be protective of those we love and provide for and take care of them. We may want to buy them things and do whatever makes them happy. However, our love can quickly shift from adoration and affection to jealousy and hate.

We may be aware of higher emotions such as compassion, forgiveness, and unconditional love, but they may be more of an abstract concept. We don't always know how to act on these more spiritual ideals.

For instance, forgiveness may seem like a weak response to being hurt and not the way to right a wrong. We may hold onto grudges and resentment for long periods of time.

We like emotions that help us feel more powerful and provide us with an increase in physical energy. Being happy, enthusiastic, and confident feels good. However, when what we experience is uncomfortable, we may repress and stuff down our feelings. If we think an emotion is bad, we may deny that we even feel it.

As an example, perhaps you believe that you shouldn't get upset with or feel uncomfortable toward those you love. When you feel angry or resentful with your partner, you may deny your feelings and stuff them down. You then intuit, feel, and attract these same feelings in others and may express them in unhealthy and damaging ways.

Through material consciousness, we are often reactive with our emotions and have a harder time processing them. We are more likely to deny and repress them and then have emotional outbursts. When we are not aware of our repressed feelings and wounds, we may blame someone or something outside of us for causing us to feel a certain way.

When our intuitive and empathic awareness is focused in material consciousness, we are attuned to the people and situations in our everyday environment. Not only do we intuit and absorb the energy of others, but we often react to and are influenced by what others are feeling as well.

For instance, if we are in the company of those who share feelings of anger or hatred toward a certain group of people, we may absorb these intense feelings. Even if we don't share their beliefs and aren't angry, we may become agitated or rude to others for no reason.

Intuiting through material consciousness can leave us feeling overwhelmed, stressed, anxious, and negative. Not only do we repress, deny, and stuff away our own uncomfortable feelings, but we also repress the difficult feelings that we intuit from others. This leads to the unhealthy cycle of attracting more of what we don't want to feel. Without insight into this destructive pattern, we continue to feel powerless and suffer.

Mental Consciousness

Through mental consciousness, we are more likely to intuit the thoughts and beliefs of others. Because the chattering voice can be especially prominent in mental consciousness, we aren't always aware of when we are intuiting. We may take on others' beliefs and ways of thinking without realizing we are doing this. This often happens in long-term relationships when partners and spouses begin to think alike and share common beliefs. It also is more likely to occur if we are lonely and want to fit into a particular group. We bond with others' thoughts and merge with their energy.

The energies of vibrationally similar thoughts and beliefs come together and form thoughtforms. People who have similar thoughts attract these thoughtforms, and their beliefs, opinions, and emotions strengthen. This, in turn, leads to attracting others with similar beliefs and opinions.

For instance, the racist and discriminatory thoughts and attitudes of some attract the similar thoughts and beliefs of others, even if they are miles and miles away. These thoughtforms then become more powerful and influential. Weak-minded people are especially vulnerable to taking on and absorbing these beliefs and adopting them as their own.

Through mental consciousness, we may also attract creative thoughtforms. These streams of energy are usually of a higher frequency and contain general and specific ideas, solutions to current problems, interesting innovations, and creative concepts. Artists, writers, innovators, inventors, and creatives of all types often receive ideas and insights from this collective creative thoughtform. When our awareness is focused in mental consciousness, we more easily intuit and absorb these creative offerings. If it is not the right time or we aren't able to pursue the ideas and concepts we receive, then the energy moves on to others.

Our ability to process our thoughts and emotions through mental consciousness is more developed than it is through material consciousness. In order to manifest what we desire, we may pay particular attention to generating and maintaining positive thoughts and emotions. Aware of the power of emotions, we do our best to stay away from negativity.

For instance, if we want to attract a loving and kind partner, we stay positive and affirm that we are attracting a loving relationship. If we become discouraged or continue to date people who do not have the qualities we are looking for, we might redouble our efforts and do our best to remain positive. Not wanting to think negative thoughts or feel less than hopeful and positive, we push these thoughts and feelings down or deny we are thinking or feeling them. We then intuit and feel these stuffed-away emotions in others, as well as attract those with repressed anger and negativity. This doomed cycle continues.

While there are many benefits we experience when we feel positive and happy, we must feel all of our emotions. When we don't feel our emotions, they don't simply go away. Instead, they become stuck in our body and energy field and we attract and intuit similar energy.

Spiritual Consciousness

Through spiritual consciousness, we attract people who align with our heart, our spirit, and our highest good. We absorb and receive divinely inspired insights, guidance, wisdom, and understanding. Unlike material and mental consciousness, we are less likely to feel and be overwhelmed by the energy of others and our environment.

However, spiritual consciousness is not an escape from difficult emotions. Instead, through spiritual awareness, our emotions transform into their highest expression. Sadness, anger, and fear, as well as joy and serenity, and all of the emotions in between, will come our way. Through spiritual consciousness, we are aware that emotions are transitory and meant to teach and guide us. They are messengers in this human dimension that help to deepen our self-awareness. Emotions and feelings inform us of what we have come here to learn, heal, and share. Pointing us toward our true spiritual nature, they show us our wounds, our stuck places, and where we need to grow and evolve.

As we allow our emotions to flow freely through us without repressing, denying, or attaching to them, our heart opens. A spiritual light emerges and leads us out of suffering and into new territory. The soft glow of the force of love is present. Our human nature wants to escape our difficult emotions. However, when we allow ourselves to feel them, our heart opens and we attract spiritual truth and healing.

When we listen within to the gentle inner voice, we intuitively receive the higher spiritual significance of what we are feeling and experiencing, as well as experience healing. For instance, we come to the understanding that grief and loss can bring us to the awareness that we can never truly lose anyone. Whatever passes out of physicality continues to live in another form. We have moments of awareness that the spirits of those we have lost through physical death are with us.

The experience of pain strips away our illusions and expectations and reveals the raw truth of our vulnerability and need for love. Pain pulls us deeper into ourselves and awakens us to our need to draw from a higher source of relief. It helps us to perceive the limitations of the purely physical realm and to allow and receive spiritual healing.

Loneliness focuses us inward and encourages us to strengthen our relationship with ourselves and with the divine. Whatever we have looked outside of ourselves for will never truly satisfy us. It is from the union of our true self and the divine that satisfying and loving connections with others emerge.

When fear grips and locks us into a frozen state and the shadows of the world cause us to cower, the force of love whispers that it is near. However, we can hear and feel this presence only when we open our heart and allow ourselves to feel. We then discover the courage and strength embedded in our heart and spirit.

Through spiritual consciousness, we escape the grasp of resentment, hatred, and hostility when we allow ourselves to feel our emotions without judgment. Something within us is in pain and needs love. Instead of focusing on another's actions or the injustice committed against us, we are led to explore more deeply what is crying out for help within our being.

Our spiritual challenge is to take responsibility for what we intuit and use this awareness to heal and evolve. Although creating safe boundaries with others and protecting ourselves from unhealthy energy is helpful, we must look within.

In the next chapter, we will explore how to identify and release repressed and stuck emotional energy and unhealed wounds. As we commit to release whatever is blocking our ability to receive the higher vibrations of spiritual consciousness, we transform.

CHAPTER 9

Clearing the Intuitive Channels

The transformation into spiritual consciousness is focused in the heart, where the human and the divine meet. Becoming aware of and releasing our stuffed-away and repressed emotions and unhealed wounds is the next step in our ascent into spiritual consciousness. As we clear our physical body and energy field of difficult and unhealthy emotions, we no longer unconsciously attract chaotic and negative energy from others and the environment. Instead, our intuitive and empathic awareness becomes the channel through which we receive higher divine frequencies.

The range of emotional sensitivity for empaths, intuitives, and sensitives is vast and deep. We can feel the highs of profound love and the depths of intense pain. Pain cuts deep into our heart and soul when another hurts us or when our sensitivity and genuine caring are misunderstood or taken advantage of. When we have been treated unfairly, ignored, mistreated, or betrayed, we may feel raw, wounded, and weak for a long time. While we can quickly and easily give to others without reservation, we don't always expose our hurt and pain to them. Revealing our wounds can feel too vulnerable, and we often prefer to go within and do our best to heal ourselves. Empaths, intuitives, and sensitives have a tendency to bury pain deep inside. It may be too difficult and overwhelming to feel the hurt. We can feel swept away by its intensity and unable to cope. We often isolate ourselves and withdraw from others when we are feeling unbalanced or uncomfortable or when we are hurting. However, suffering in silence and distancing ourselves from those who can give us the comfort and understanding we need intensifies feelings of being different and alone.

The heart is the multidimensional emotional center for empaths, intuitives, and sensitives. In both human and spiritual terms, the heart gives us life. The heart circulates blood through our physical system, which in turn supplies us with oxygen and nutrients. On an energetic level, the heart channels the divine energy of the force of love throughout our mind, body, and spirit. It also helps us feel and process the loving and not-so-loving emotions that we encounter in our relationships and daily life.

Our tendency to shield and protect our heart is instinctual. As empaths, intuitives, and sensitives, we are accustomed to feeling and absorbing waves of emotions, thoughts, and energy. Feeling the emotions of others doesn't always feel good. A fair amount of the time, it can feel pretty lousy. Feeling our own and another's fear, anger, or negativity might motivate us to close our heart and do all we can not to feel. We may attempt to shield ourselves when we experience the onslaught of absorbed emotions. Feeling the suffering of others is no small matter. It's difficult to feel our own pain, and taking on the difficult emotional energy of others is exhausting and unhealthy. Closing our heart may seem to be the only way to protect ourselves and control what we feel and intuit. We may want to avoid or get away from whatever or whoever we view as the source of our discomfort.

While we may try to protect ourselves from intuiting the difficult emotional energy of others, these feelings often reflect our own stuffed-away emotions. The energy we intuit in another is usually similar to our own repressed emotional energy. When we are triggered and have a strong reaction to the energy we feel and intuit from another, it is often our own unconscious emotions and feelings that cause us distress.

For instance, let's say you intuit and empathically feel a friend's anger. When you ask her if she is angry, she tells you that she is feeling taken advantage of at work. She admits that she is feeling frustrated but doesn't feel there is anything she can do to change the situation. Later that day, you find yourself feeling unappreciated by your husband. Anger wells up within you. Even though you've tried to put these feelings behind you, you have been denying your anger. You realize that the anger you intuited about your friend is similar to your feelings toward your husband.

Our stuffed-away wounds and emotions emit a signal that attracts similar energy in others. While the emotions, pain, and wounds that we are conscious of attract like energy, the unconscious and forgotten stored-away energy within us is the more powerful magnet. We may believe that the intuited energy of another is causing us to feel overwhelmed, burdened, negative, or stressed. However, while another person's energy might be anxious or negative, it is our energetic reaction to it that amplifies our discomfort.

Other people's energy can stimulate and encourage the stuffed-away emotions and wounds within us to surface. Feeling the intensity of these forgotten and unprocessed feelings as they come into our awareness can be confusing. When we have a strong reaction to what we intuit, this as a sign that something in us needs our attention and healing.

The Origin of Our Energy Blocks

Our unhealed wounds and ungrieved losses and repressed emotions form inner energy blocks that keep us from clear sensing, intuiting, and feeling. Stuck energy inhibits our ability to soak in the beneficial flow of the force of love. Energy blocks create tension and anxiety in our mind and body and keep us from opening our heart to higher vibrations.

Repressing and stuffing down painful emotions and wounds often begins in childhood. When we are young, we aren't able to understand our emotions and put what we feel into words. Empathic, intuitive, and sensitive children are often misunderstood and labeled as difficult, unruly, or problematic. We are prone to expressing and releasing the uncomfortable emotional energy that builds up within us through our behavior. Often scolded and punished for these actions, we learn to stuff our feelings down and deny our emotional needs. Because we don't always know why we feel the way we do, we are at a loss as to how to deal with our emotions.

Childhood trauma and challenging situations and experiences can be soul-deadening, especially for young intuitives, empaths, and sensitives. We rarely are able to fully feel and process what is happening, and we may shut down, bury our emotions, and go into a state of shock. When we are unable to process experiences that cause us pain, confusion, or fear, the trauma gets stored in our heart, stomach, liver, and other places in our physical body and energy field. Unprocessed emotional energy remains within us with the same intensity it had when we experienced it. When the emotions and unhealed wounds that we have stuffed down begin to surface, the potency of what we feel may take us by surprise. We also may be confused as to where these uncomfortable feelings are coming from.

Difficult past repressed emotions need to be felt, released, and healed. Just as our physical body works to release such things as toxins and viruses, so does our energy body desire to let go of past pain and stagnant and repressed emotions. Unfortunately, we don't usually recognize it when past emotions surface to be healed and released. When difficult emotions seem to come out of nowhere, we may do our best to ignore what we are feeling or assume that we are intuitively feeling another's energy. We may push our emotions back down and attempt to get our mind off them through such things as eating, shopping, playing video games, drinking, or other addictive types of activity. Until we allow our repressed emotions and unhealed wounds to surface and feel them, they stay within us.

Identifying Repressed Emotions and Unhealed Wounds

Here are some signs that indicate the presence of unhealed and repressed emotions and wounds embedded in the physical body and/or energy field:

- I feel as if my purpose is to be of service to others. But when I am with those in need, it feels like I absorb and feel their suffering and difficulties.
- When I open my heart, my feelings are easily hurt by my friends and family.
- I feel lonely most of the time and want to connect with others. Yet when I am in social situations, I get anxious and feel overwhelmed by the energy of others.

- Thinking positive thoughts and having gratitude doesn't seem to work for me. I feel better for a while, then feel like crap again.

- I used to be intuitive and notice synchronicities and I want to get this magic back.

- Why do I always end up in relationships with people who abandon me? I try so hard, but it doesn't seem to make a difference.

- I get such negative vibes from others. What's wrong with people? I try to be positive, but I always seem to find myself surrounded by people who view the cup as half-empty.

To release the wounds, blocks, and repressed emotional energy within our physical body and energy field, we need to feel them. This process is uncomplicated and natural. However, because it brings up uncomfortable memories and pain that we don't want to feel, we resist the process.

For the most part, energy flows through us undetected. Just as we aren't aware of our breath unless we focus on it, we also don't notice the subtle sensations and feelings that continually move though us. The easiest way to become more aware of what we are feeling is to focus on our breath and observe the subtle feelings and sensations as they come and go.

The following exercise will help you to tune into and better identify inner repressed emotional energy, unhealed wounds, and accumulated energy.

....

EXERCISE
Healing Scan to Release Repressed and Stuffed-Away Emotions

Lie down in a comfortable and quiet place where you will not be disturbed. Close your eyes and take a long, deep breath. Release any stress and tension through the exhale.

Continue to breathe and relax. Send relaxing breath through your entire body, and exhale any stress and tension.

To scan your body and energy field, draw your attention to the area above your head. Slowly move your awareness down through your body and in the space about twelve inches outside of your body.

When you feel tightness, tension, a knot, or emptiness, or if you are drawn to a specific area, pause. Focus your awareness there and become receptive. Just listen, feel, and observe. Don't try to figure out what you are receiving or what is happening. Be passive yet alert and receptive. Keep breathing and be patient.

When we initially move our awareness through our body, we might not feel any identifiable feelings or stuck or repressed energy. If this happens, continue to breathe and continue to scan from the top of your head to the soles of your feet. When you become aware of and feel a distinct but perhaps subtle area of tension, tightness, emptiness, or denseness, pause.

Take a long, deep, relaxing inhale and release any stress through the exhale.

What is the emotion and feeling connected to this energy?

Energy responds to our inquiries. Instead of using words, energy often speaks to us through sensations, feelings, memories, thoughts, and sometimes images. However, the most important connection we can make with this energy is to feel it. Although it can be interesting to be aware of the origin of the energy that has generated this wound or repressed and blocked energy, don't focus on this.

You might begin to feel many different emotions. Some feelings may be vague and subtle, while others will be stronger and more intense. Unhealed wounds may bring up feelings of sadness, anger, or helplessness. Most of us will tend to want to unconsciously avoid and try to skip over the important step of feeling. Remember, this is why and how the energy became lodged and blocked to begin with.

We might also feel very little. Stuffed-down and repressed emotions and wounds are often frozen, and it may take some time for them to thaw out. Sometimes the energy is dense or hard and blocked. It cannot speak to us, and we may have a difficult time feeling it. If you sense a frozen or blocked area of energy, breathe and send it love and compassion. Continue to listen, feel, and sense any messages.

If it doesn't feel as if you receive a response from the stuck energy you are focusing on, don't be concerned. Send a loving message to the repressed emotions or wounds that it is safe to surface. Open your heart and know that the powerful force of love is present. Eventually the emotions will begin to surface. Pay attention when they do, and resist the tendency to automatically push them back down.

All we have to do to release the energy of repressed emotions and unhealed wounds is feel. This allows the stored-up emotional pain to be released. As we feel the emotions, they dissipate and are no longer bound up within us.

Allow yourself to fully feel, even if you are feeling confusion or doubt and your emotions don't make sense. Take your time with this process. Be patient and attentive to the emotions, feelings, and old wounds that surface.

When you feel that you have released as much of the pent-up, repressed pain as you can at this time, continue to relax and breathe. Imagine the force of love flowing from your heart and throughout your physical body and energy field. Allow it to gather in the places where there has been tightness, tension, a knot, or a heavy feeling. Breathe into these places and send love and compassion. Pause, rest, and feel. When you are ready, write down any insights or new awareness you received.

Tuning into and becoming conscious of our repressed emotional energy and unhealed wounds is a process that occurs over time. As our emotions and unhealed wounds begin to thaw out, we might feel detached from them or only faintly feel them. Be patient. Once we become aware of stuck emotions, they will begin to work themselves into our awareness. As emotions surface, we may have random spells of feeling vulnerable, moody, weepy, or sad. Allow this process to take as long as it needs. As emotions surface, remember that these are the feelings that we stuffed away. However difficult it is to feel our uncomfortable emotions, as we feel them, they are released. What we don't acknowledge and feel disrupts the flow of the force of love through our body, mind, and spirit and manifests in disharmony in our day-to-day circumstances.

To accelerate the emotional detox that occurs when we let go of repressed emotions and unhealed wounds, drink lots of water, eat fresh fruits and vegetables, and get a lot of sleep and rest. Journaling can encourage intuitive insights and more emotions to surface and provide us with even deeper insights. Repressed emotions and unhealed wounds often surface when we are sleeping. Pay attention to your dreams and write them down. This will help to move energy out of the body. Physical activity such as yoga, running, or walking in nature can be helpful. Being close to water or spending time in a hot tub or steam room encourages more emotional detoxing. If it feels as if there is energy that is hard to access because it is blocked or trapped, massage therapy, acupuncture, or another type of bodywork can help to stimulate deeper emotional clearing.

When We Get Triggered

For empathic, intuitive, and highly sensitive people, absorbing or sensing the emotional energy of another or a situation often takes us out of present time and into the past. The energy that we intuit from others can trigger and activate past pain and what we have attempted to put behind us. It isn't always obvious when past memories and stuffed-away emotions and unresolved issues come to the surface We often experience our past unhealed wounds and difficult emotions to the same degree that we originally experienced them. Even if trauma and difficulties occurred years earlier or when we were quite young, we may experience the emotions with the same intensity that we first felt them.

For instance, perhaps you sense or intuit that a friend is going through something difficult. When you reach out and ask if there is anything wrong, she tells you that everything is fine. Still, your empathic awareness tells you differently. You become increasingly stressed as you wonder how you can best help her. The inner pressure to do something escalates, and you find yourself worried and concerned about her.

As you contemplate what you can do to help your friend, an unexpected intuitive insight comes to you. The feelings and concern you are feeling about your friend remind you of the worry and stress you often felt with your mother when you were young. She often seemed to be sad and distant. Although you felt your mother's feelings, you didn't know what to do to help her. She would try to assure you that everything was fine. Still, in your heart you felt this wasn't true. Eventually your mother sank into a depression and became physically ill. She shut you out and resisted your attempts to try to comfort or help her. For years you wondered if there was something you could have done differently. Although you wanted to help your mother, you never were able to. Although this is a memory from long ago, it intensifies your frustration and adds to your worry and stress about your friend.

When the feelings and energy that we absorb, sense, or intuit from others trigger our repressed emotions and wounds, we don't always have the clear awareness that this is happening. We might look around wondering who or what is giving off the sad or negative energy that we feel. Our mind goes into overdrive in an attempt to figure out what is causing our distress. Because there doesn't seem to be anything currently happening in our life that has generated these feelings, we assume that we are intuiting them from someone else. However, it is likely that both the energy of another and our own repressed feelings are causing our discomfort. Our unhealed wounds and unresolved issues have been intuitively triggered, and this is what is creating havoc within us.

For instance, Lia, a client of mine, told me that during a heart opening meditation in her yoga class, she immediately began to feel overwhelmed with confusing and difficult emotions. The emotional intensity she felt was powerful. Lia is an empath, and she felt as if she was absorbing these emotions from others. Because of this experience, she wasn't sure she wanted to go back to the class.

Intuitive and empathic feelings and thoughts come and go, so much so that it isn't always possible to know their origin. Too often we make assumptions as to why we suddenly feel surprising feelings and sensations. In our desire to better understand the thoughts and feelings that don't seem to make sense, we may jump to premature conclusions that may not be correct.

As an example, when my friend Ryan first met Claire, he could feel her pain. He felt an unexpected feeling of sadness when they first talked. Although Claire didn't mention any recent losses or issues, he was sure that she was going through emotional difficulties.

However, Ryan misunderstood the source of the emotions he felt. Claire triggered the unhealed loss that Ryan had experienced with a past girlfriend who looked similar to Claire. While Claire may have been sad and he may have empathically felt it, the intensity of the emotions came from his own repressed emotions.

Subtle intuitive stimuli, such as coincidences, empathic sensitivity, and even scents, can trigger the emergence of repressed and hidden feelings and thoughts. The intuitive sensations and empathic energy we receive may cause us to become concerned that a particular person, situation, or activity is not good for us. Sometimes the energy that we intuitively absorb is overwhelming and we cannot process or even put it into words. It may seem that we have no control over what we are experiencing and being influenced by. We may blame others for making us tired, anxious, or worried and feel cursed by our sensitivity and at its mercy. In our perceived powerlessness, we do our best to get away from the people, situations, and events that we believe are creating the problem. It's no wonder we mistrust or deny our intuition, close our heart, and isolate ourselves from others. Why would anyone want to be continually soaking in painful or negative emotions or overwhelmed with energy?

As an example, perhaps a friend says something with no intent or desire to hurt you, but you take it personally. The offhand remark stirs up anger and pain. You wonder why your friend is being so insensitive and mean. No matter what they say to try to let you know that they did not mean to hurt your feelings, the remark still stings.

When we continually find ourselves in the company of others or in situations where we absorb unsettling or negative energy, this is a sign that something within us needs healing. If we don't release our repressed energy, we keep attracting and absorbing the lower vibrations we are trying to get away from. We don't see others or situations as they are. Instead, they are a reflection of our consciousness. Having repressed emotional energy and wounds doesn't mean that we are inherently negative, toxic, or flawed. The energy that we are intuiting is a mirror that has come to shine a light on what is blocking our ability to receive higher loving and wise vibrations.

Signs of Surfacing Repressed Emotions

The optimal time to release and clear stuck emotions is when they have been activated and begin to surface. Our intuitive energy sensitivity draws to us the people and situations that are similar to our repressed emotions. Notice when you feel uncomfortable emotions. We become so accustomed to ignoring and minimizing what we are feeling that we often push aside and ignore our emotions. Unfortunately, they don't go far. Once we are aware of and feel the emotions and energy that we have stuffed away, we heal.

Here are some signs that our stuffed-down emotions and unhealed wounds are being triggered:

- We have intense and out-of-place emotional reactions to common, everyday experiences.

- We relive past emotional situations over and over in our head, thinking about what we might have done or said differently.

- We experience overwhelming and overblown emotional reactions to unexpected changes and inconveniences.

- We intuit emotions such as anger, grief, stress, and resentment from others without realizing that these are emotions we often feel ourselves.

- We wake up at night with intense emotions or have dreams that stir up confusing feelings.

- We experience the sudden surfacing of uncomfortable feelings while doing mundane activities such as driving, exercising, cleaning, or cooking.

- We often sense that others are out to get us or are intentionally trying to hurt us or stir up trouble.

- We feel a jumble of emotions when we try to meditate or listen within.

- We have a recurrent fear of being treated unfairly or victimized.

- We have frequent issues with anxiety, panic attacks, overeating, or other addictions or with physical aches and pains, disease, and illness.

....

PRACTICE
Feel Emotions as They Surface

If you suspect that stuffed-down emotional energy is being triggered and surfacing, remind yourself that this is an opportunity to heal. Notice and become more conscious of emotions that surface that seem out of proportion to what is happening. Here are some examples:

- A friend asks to reschedule a lunch date and you are hurt and disappointed. You are upset for days and contemplate ending the friendship.

- Your son doesn't seem overly enthusiastic when he opens his birthday gift, and you are riddled with sadness and guilt. You immediately buy him more gifts even though you can't afford it.

- A waiter in a restaurant brings you the wrong order. Personally slighted, you scold the waiter and demand to speak to the manager. You create a scene and embarrass your family.

Do your best to feel and observe whatever you feel in these types of situations. Acknowledge and name your feelings as they surface. Catch yourself if you find that you automatically dismiss your emotions or blame others for them. Give your emotions space to surface.

Don't push down or try to minimize what you are feeling. Sometimes we feel guilty or overly sensitive or believe that something is wrong with us because of what we are feeling. Don't judge yourself. Something within you is hurting, and this is worthy of your attention.

When you notice yourself feeling intense emotions that are out of proportion to what is happening, take a deep breath and allow whatever you feel to surface. Feel your emotions fully. Don't push them away or ignore them. Feel them in all their intensity. Even if this feels difficult and uncomfortable, don't judge yourself or the emotions. You will get through this.

Strong and overwhelming emotions are usually an accumulation of past wounds and feelings that have been with us for a long time. We initially buried them within because we didn't believe that we could feel them. It hurt too much and felt too painful to endure. We might unconsciously feel that we still cannot handle them. Remember, whatever caused these feelings is over and is in the past. You are safe and can feel what is surfacing.

As you feel the emotions and wounds, they dissipate and heal. Open your heart and allow the force of love to flow through you.

If you are in a situation or place where you cannot process the emotions that are being triggered, commit to working through this process soon. Don't let it go for too long. Make some time to be alone in a place where you can allow the feelings to surface.

....

EXERCISE
Triggering Buried Emotions
and Unhealed Wounds

Have you ever been surprised by your reaction to a situation or event or by something someone did or said? Buried emotions and unhealed wounds can surface at inappropriate or awkward moments. Sometimes the emotions can burn with such intensity that we say or do something that we later regret. It's also likely that our emotions will simmer within us and create stress, anxiety, or depression. Unfortunately, we aren't always aware that past repressed emotions and old wounds are at the core of what we are feeling and experiencing.

Instead of waiting for someone or something to trigger your repressed emotions and unhealed wounds, you can invite them to surface.

When you are feeling calm, rested, and centered, imagine a situation, person, or memory that stirs up an emotional response in you. What brings up strong feelings such as anger, sadness, or fear? Are there events in the past that still arouse strong feelings? When do you feel emotionally out of control and reactive? You can invoke these feelings by recalling past memories.

When you begin to feel the emotions more acutely, ask yourself, "Where in my physical body or energy field does the energy of these emotions feel the most intense?"

Place your hand on the part of your body where energy of the emotions feels the strongest. This is where the repressed emotional energy or unhealed wound may be lodged. There might be more than one area within your body that is storing this energy. Place your hand on the area where the emotion feels the most intense. If you aren't able to identify a specific location, place your hands on your heart or solar plexus.

Breathe and feel the energy of the emotions. Feel whatever surfaces, and do your best to identify your emotions as they surface.

As you feel the feelings, say something like, "As I feel the energy of these difficult emotions, it dissipates and goes into the light," or "I am releasing these difficult feelings into the force of love."

Continue to breathe and open your heart, mind, and body to the force of love. Let this love move through you and help you release difficult and stressful emotions.

It can be helpful to participate in some form of action or activity to further release repressed emotions. Here are a few things that can be helpful when clearing out repressed emotions and pain:

- Talk about your emotions with someone who is safe, nonjudgmental, and loving.
- Paint or work with clay, crayons, or any artistic medium.
- Write, scribble, journal, or create poetry.
- Walk, run, swim, dance, or lift weights.
- Take a yoga or movement class.
- Paint or redecorate your living space.
- Garden, plant, weed, or go fruit picking.
- Volunteer to help others in some way.
- Take up a new hobby.

- Do something positive for yourself that you've always wanted to do.

- Take a sauna or steam bath or get bodywork, acupuncture, or a massage.

- Listen to your heart and gut for ways to take care of yourself.

- Establish safe boundaries for yourself with others in certain situations.

- Say no if something isn't right for you.

Freedom from Pain

We tend to do everything we can to avoid uncomfortable feelings and emotions. Through material consciousness, pain has the power to control our lives and condemn us to unhappiness. We may feel victimized, taken advantage of, and unfairly treated. We often blame ourselves, others, and circumstances for our bad luck and misfortune. Pain is to be avoided.

Through spiritual consciousness, pain doesn't come into our lives to punish us or as a result of negative thoughts or victimization. Instead, its message is transcendence. Pain wakes us up. Many who are spiritual, intuitive, and empathic have experienced a lot of pain and loss in life. It is often when we are in the depths of despair, loneliness, and suffering that we instinctively reach out to the unseen. Although the invisible presence is usually quiet, subtle, and barely detectable, something in our heart and soul moves us to open up and trust it. We sense and intuitively know that there is something beyond the physical world, and we want it to bring us relief and comfort. Suffering often motivates our spiritual journey.

Pain and suffering push and prod us into change and new perspectives. Through spiritual consciousness, we can use our suffering to open to a new understanding about ourselves and life. We can become aware of where we are stuck and resisting growth. However, suffering is not sent to us by the divine. It is our own soul that creates the circumstances that will best help us to evolve, heal, and come into our full potential.

Our repressed, toxic, and unhealed emotions and wounds need our love. What feels unbearable can be the vehicle through which we allow ourselves to receive love and higher spiritual awareness. Feeling and releasing energy patterns and stuck and repressed emotions is spiritual work. Our resistance to this process can be deep and hidden. Feeling the waves of repressed and stuffed-away emotions as they surface isn't easy. We might try our best to distract ourselves or become frustrated with what feels like a lack of progress or discernible positive change. We want the process to be easier, and we can convince ourselves that feeling our feelings is not helpful or healing. The spiritual path, we reason, should be one of solace and joy.

When the healing path becomes difficult, we have a choice. We can retreat to the empty spiritual clichés or we can free ourselves. If we want true freedom, we have to accept the often rigorous challenges of the spiritual path. It doesn't steer us away from our suffering, but through it. As long as we view our feelings and experiences as more powerful than we are, they bind and control us.

Be gentle with your stuck energy and all of the tight knots and blocks that you discover within. They need your compassion and loving attention. Most likely these pockets of fear, trauma, overwhelm, and grief have been with you for a long time. Left unattended, they have taken root within. They are preventing the inner free flow of high-vibration energy that is necessary for optimal mental, emotional, physical, and spiritual health. Like a logjam in a river, these knots and spots of tightness and tension become stagnant, pouring energy into our fears, negativity, stress, anxiety, and grief.

The following exercise can help you embrace your inner stuffed-away energy in loving kindness to yourself.

··

EXERCISE
Dear Suffering

Send a message to the dormant inner pain within you that it is safe to emerge and be felt and released. Writing an encouraging letter to the stuffed-away emotions facilitates connection and gentle release.

Here is an example:

Dear Anger, Fear, or Grief (or other emotion),

I know that you have been hiding inside of me for a long time. Sometimes I feel you, and it scares me. There seems to be so much intensity locked up inside of me. I'm afraid that if I let these feelings surface, I'll be overwhelmed and fall apart or maybe lash out at people who don't deserve my anger. Also, I'm afraid that underneath this anger, there is a lot of sadness and grief. I feel alone with all the sadness inside of me.

I think my constant tiredness and health issues are due to the repressed emotions, and I want to let them go. I understand why I stuffed these feelings down and know that there has been a lot to be angry, fearful, and sad about throughout my life, especially in my childhood. Help me to let go.

When you have finished writing, take some long, deep, relaxing breaths, releasing any stress and tension on the

exhale. Breathe, relax, and listen within for loving and
wise guidance and whispers of support.

Our unhealed wounds and stuck emotions need our help and
attention. The tightness and blocks in our energy field are potent.
When we nurture our pain and wounds with love and understanding, we soften and the force of love flows freely. The energy of emotions such as grief, trauma, and fear that has been stored within
loosens its grip on us. It becomes like the mist of a summer shower
or the spray of an ocean breeze, absorbed by the light.

As our spiritual consciousness strengthens, we begin to recognize that we are never truly alone. We are connected to a larger
divine and celestial force that is always present. We are often
drawn into the darkness to see the light. As we allow a higher
divine force of love to move through us, the beauty of our soul is
ignited.

The spiritual challenge is to open our heart and feel. When
our heart is open, we breathe deeply and allow energy to move
through us. We feel our emotions, but they don't stick to us and
linger in our heart, mind, and body. We let them go. When we
stuff down and repress negative and unhealthy emotions, they
are like poison to our system. They harm our body, mind, and
spirit. An open heart allows our emotions and the intuited and
absorbed energy of others to pass through us. Although we still
feel our own and others' emotions and energy, it doesn't trigger
unhealed wounds and trapped emotions. What we feel and intuit
moves through us. We are free.

CHAPTER 10

The Vast and Deep
Love of the Empath

There is a compelling and penetrating soulful drive within empaths and the intuitive and sensitive to love and be a ray of light, hope, inspiration, and healing to others. Refining our ability to love ourselves and others defines our journey into spiritual consciousness. The next step in ascending into spiritual consciousness is to examine how we love. As we integrate the force of love into our body, mind, and spirit, the way we love ourselves and others may also need to transform.

Intuitive, empathic, and sensitive people are often drawn to those in need. Intertwined with our deep intuitive sensitivity is the desire to be of service. We may be able to quickly sense pain and grief in others, and we seek out ways to help and heal them. When someone is hurt, our love is called into action and moves through us like the notes through an instrument. The feeling of love coursing through our heart and soul is immensely satisfying. We love and give and it feels good. While our desire to love and care for others is noble, it can also be a source of confusion, misunderstanding, and, at times, pain. Most empaths, intuitives, and sensitives experience a wider and deeper range of emotions than others. This is integral to our nature, and we simply cannot *not* feel and intuit. The feelings, thoughts, and energy of others can affect us in subtle, unconscious, or overt ways.

Although everyone is influenced and affected by energy to some degree, empaths and the intuitive and sensitive are more likely to be aware of the energy vibes in others and in our surroundings. We are attuned to the different textures of feelings, sensations, and qualities that energy embodies. Sometimes the energy of another feels light and inviting, and other times it can be heavy and off-putting. This is true for situations and environments as well. Specific locations often hold energy imprints that are not always positive and pleasant.

Despite the uncomfortable vibes and feelings that we intuit from others, our inner well of empathy is vast and deep. When we feel another's sadness, distress, anger, or other similar emotions, our inner barometer often steers us toward them and not away. Our desire to help, give to, and be with others who are struggling or going through emotional challenges draws us to their side.

These kind of experiences may be familiar to you:

- Something feels off about Leo's vibe. It feels like he's pushing me away. But I'm not going anywhere. I'm here for him.
- It feels like Maggie and Trevor may be dealing with some issues. I can feel the friction. I still plan on going to the beach with them though. Maybe I can be helpful.
- Keke always looks happy, but I feel her sadness. I'll keep loving her and do my best to be there for her.

• I feel like Samuel has more talent that he is aware of. He could be at the top of his field. I wish there was some way that I could help him see and know this.

While we are able to intuit insights and empathically feel another's energy, we don't always know what to do with the information we receive. Intuitive and empathic sensitivity stirs our heart, and we do our best to understand others and be a source of strength and love for them. Unfortunately, we don't always take care of ourselves and pay attention to our needs in the process.

We might be able to feel and know what others who are miles away are feeling or experiencing. It's not just family, friends, and coworkers who are at a distance that we intuitively connect with. Empaths and the intuitive and sensitive often intuit and absorb the energy of casual acquaintances and may become overstimulated by crowds or just by being in a public place. Some empaths, intuitives, and sensitives can watch or listen to a news broadcast and feel the despair and suffering of others even though they are thousands of miles away. Many are sensitive to the pain experienced by animals who are mistreated or raised in deplorable conditions.

When the intuited feeling, knowing, and sensing that we receive becomes too much, we may try to turn off our intuition. Stuffing away or repressing the intuited and empathic feelings and sensations that bombard us or creating distance, both emotionally and physically, from others may seem to be our only remedies. Although separation from others and closing our heart might reduce some of the energetic overload we experience, this can take a toll on our psyche. Being empathic and intuitively sensitive can be lonely. Shutting down our receptivity takes a toll. When we attempt to detach from our intuitive and empathic awareness, our heart closes and the rich energy of the force of love is stifled and blocked. This may cause us to lose the emotional connections we have with others and weaken our trust in ourselves and a higher presence and power. Our fear and stress increase, and we may feel powerless and at the mercy of forces we don't understand.

How Empaths Bond with Others

Even though feeling, sensing, and absorbing the energy of others can be challenging, being empathic, intuitive, and sensitive is a blessing and a sign of a natural affinity to spiritual consciousness. As much as we might want to turn off our intuitive, empathic, and sensitive nature, it's not possible. Our spirit has brought our intuitive and empathic abilities to the forefront for a purpose. Something powerful within is at work.

Empathic and intuitive perception extends beyond the five senses and logic and reason and into the heart and soulful awareness. We are not superficial and are rarely attracted to another because of how much money they make, their occupation, or other external qualities. More attuned to soul connections, we crave relationships that extend into the higher sublime vibrations. We would rather open our heart and allow another into our being than make small talk. Love flows through the veins of empaths and the intuitively sensitive.

Through material consciousness, we often feel love along a continuum of varying states such as desire, jealousy, compassion, and caring, and all of the emotions in between. It is in the higher evolved states of awareness that we experience love as more than an emotion or a feeling. Through spiritual consciousness, the empath, intuitive, and sensitive evolves and embodies the divine states of love and becomes a channel through which this higher love flows. This is the love that heals, nurtures, transforms, and creates. Wordless and often undefinable, love is our compass and often leads us to the people and situations where we can have a positive impact. Love moves through our soul and wakes, stirs, and motivates us.

The empath, intuitive, and sensitive bonds with others through the heart, spirit, and energy field. This bond of love is more than feeling, longing, and desire. It is the intermingling of the energy of souls with one another and a synergy that goes beyond emotional and physical boundaries. Divine love is the strongest energy that exists and the celestial creative force that nurtures and sustains us. It can be electrifying and energizing, soothing, enlightening, and simply comforting. When we love someone, we open our heart and receive their essence; our love energies intermingle and we form a bond. In a mutually satisfying love relationship, we are supported and strengthened by another's love and our partner is supported by ours. We give and we receive. Every relationship has issues to work through and important lessons and challenges that help us grow and evolve. When we truly love another, we are not dependent on them and they are not dependent on us. We give and share the higher love that sustains us.

Unfortunately, not all relationships provide us with a healthy exchange of energy. Integrating our soulful awareness of love into our everyday, mundane human experience is challenging. Empaths and the intuitive and sensitive are naturally compassionate and heart-centered and find fulfillment in contributing in ways that uplift and affect others in positive ways. We may be romantically attracted to someone because we intuitively feel and sense that we can help and heal them. When we feel that someone needs us, we love without reservation. Many of us have been preoccupied with others' needs for so long that over-giving is normal. However, continually bolstering another's inner emptiness and low self-esteem isn't healthy for them or us. When we feel we need to be the source of love for someone, we create an energetic imbalance. We convey to others the unspoken message that they are emotionally inadequate. Eventually they will become resentful of their dependency on our love.

Despite our elevated communion with the energy of love, we often find ourselves drawn to those who would take advantage and use us for their personal benefit. Some sense our open heart and willingness to give. Empaths and the intuitively sensitive can focus and shower love and attention on another without reservation. We see others in ways that they may never have been seen or known before. To someone who isn't used to this kind of attention, this can feel seductive, compelling, and frightening all at the same time.

When we are out of touch with our own emotional needs, we are most vulnerable to being taken advantage of by those who are wounded, in need, misunderstood, or lost. When we haven't allowed our repressed and stuffed-away emotions to surface and have unhealed wounds, we are prone to attracting broken souls. Our repressed pain often draws to us those with similar wounds, and we mistakenly assume this is a true love connection. When we share emotional patterns with another, we feel an unconscious familiarity. At first meeting, it may seem as if we share a soul connection or have known someone all our life. Being in the company of someone with repressed emotions and unhealed wounds that are similar to our own can feel comfortable and confusing at the same time. Unfortunately, this leads us into relationships with those who are not capable of loving us.

When we open our heart and soul to others, we may begin to feel their emotions. We absorb the worries, burdens, and stress of others and often become overwhelmed by their energy. However, feeling and intuiting what another is experiencing doesn't take away or diminish their problems, issues, and emotional difficulties. Instead, when we absorb the distressed energy of another, it magnifies and strengthens this energy, both for ourselves and for others. We may believe that if we are able to intuit and become aware of another's emotions, problems, and pain, then it is our responsibility to help them in some way. This can lead to exhaustion, depression, and feeling emotionally, spiritually, mentally, and physically depleted. Even if we have let go of a lot of our past unhealthy emotional baggage, we may still attract those in pain.

To understand the drive toward those who might use, harm, and take advantage of us, it's necessary to understand the heart of an empath, intuitive, and sensitive. Most empaths and the intuitively sensitive know the sting of pain all too well. We may have felt different and odd throughout our entire lives. Some have endured years of feeling misunderstood or being bullied or abused in some form in childhood or as an adult. Our love wishes to be expressed and shared. When we feel another's pain and suffering, our heart spontaneously responds.

From a young age, we likely have done our best to help and heal others. Most empaths and the intuitive and sensitive are the emotional barometer within their family system. We are the ones who feel what others are feeling and often unknowingly act this out through our behavior. We are the black sheep who are more sensitive to and affected by the unspoken energy within the home. Dysfunctional families are especially challenging for an empath.

Empathic and intuitive children often unconsciously absorb their family members' sadness, grief, stress, and other emotions. Many are not aware that they are doing this and are chronically moody and suffer from stomach problems, headaches, and other physical, mental, and emotional issues. The unconscious intuitive and empathic pattern of absorbing the pain and suffering of others continues into adulthood. Taking on the burdens of another becomes second nature.

When we grow up in an environment where we intuit and feel others' emotions, we unconsciously dismiss our own needs. We sense and feel what others are feeling and do our best to soothe, heal, and be there for them. Anticipating others' wants and needs and doing our best to provide for them comes easily. Many empaths are unaware that it is possible to help, heal, and love others without taking on their energy.

Healing Our Relationships

The soul impulse to express love as comfort and healing instinctively moves us, and we give freely to those in need. The pure energy of love often bypasses our more conscious and rational self. Its power moves through our heart and soul and we follow. Love is a healing balm, and we are convinced that there is no wound that it cannot mend.

There are those who sense our vulnerability and open heart and either knowingly or unknowingly try to form an unhealthy attachment to us. Some may resent our positivity and openness and take us for fools. They may have no qualms about draining our energy and using us in ways that cause confusion and even pain. Surprisingly, they might justify their behavior as teaching us a lesson in not being naive or a similar excuse. Empaths, intuitives, and the sensitive often attract individuals with narcissistic tendencies. These wounded and ego-centered individuals lack empathy and awareness of others' needs and feelings. With a need for constant attention and admiration, they feel entitled to use and abuse others for their purposes.

The desire to heal and love can cause us to misread what is happening in a relationship and how it might be adversely affecting us. We might see the beautiful, vulnerable, and positive in others even when they cannot see it themselves. We may want to be the mirror through which another can see their true self. Unfortunately, our desire to help is often not appreciated or wanted. Not everyone is ready and willing to change and heal. It is a personal choice that we all must make on our own. No matter how much we may love another and see their inner beauty, we cannot help them if they do not recognize the need for it. Many with unhealed wounds are not ready or lack the courage to pursue their own healing and are unable to open their heart. They may resent our ability to love and not want to be reminded of what they cannot feel and give.

Even when our connection with someone causes us pain, we might continue to soldier on. We don't want to let down, abandon, or be the source of another's pain and feelings of rejection. When there is friction in a relationship, we might blame ourselves for it and continue to be mistreated or ignored. Those who are wounded often become numb to others' feelings and needs. They have covered up their emotions and needs for so long that they are no longer able to feel and respond to others with care and sensitivity. They may attempt to make up for their self-loathing and feelings of inadequacy and lack by latching onto the positive and loving energy of others. Some have an unconscious drive that pushes them to seek out and attempt to manipulate and take advantage of the love they sense within us. They may desire love and seek to destroy it at the same time.

Focusing on another's needs keeps us from being vulnerable and acknowledging our own needs. The purpose of our journey is not to avoid and close our heart to those who are suffering and in pain. Instead, it is to recognize that all healing comes from within. We can have compassion for and encourage others to open to the force of love within their heart, mind, and soul. However, it is essential that we do the same for ourselves. Taking care of ourselves and creating boundaries allows us to express the vulnerability and softness of our heart. It is only those who can truly love us and treat us with respect that we allow into the innermost and intimate place in our heart.

If you are in a romantic relationship or close friendship with or attracted to someone who is emotionally wounded, do your best to discern if they are actively engaged in their healing journey. Do they recognize their wounds and actively seek ways to heal? Do they deny and minimize their pain and express it in unhealthy ways? Are they engaged in an active addiction to numb their feelings and emotions? What steps are they taking to take care of themselves?

Be honest about your motivation for wanting to help and give to someone you are in a relationship with. Ask yourself, "Do I feel that I can give another the love they feel they lack? Do I minimize my own needs? Can I freely share the issues and concerns that affect me with those I am close to? Do I feel that I will be supported and listened to? Am I focused on another's potential instead of their current situation and level of self-awareness?"

Recognize that in loving another, we have a responsibility to give the highest expression of love and care that we are capable of. We also must allow and receive the love and care of others.

How Energy Cords Form

In our desire to love and help heal others, we may unknowingly enter into unhealthy energy connections. Energy cords are invisible lines of energy that attach people to one another. When there is an imbalance of give-and-take and control and need in a relationship, energy cords form. Instead of connecting to the highest source of love, we mutually attach to each other. Energy cords keep us bound to each other in an unhealthy way. Usually one partner is over-giving and the other is over-receiving. While the partner who is receiving the life force energy of the other may feel healthy and vibrant and be full of energy, the other becomes exhausted and drained. Often the partner receiving energy may become more dominant and controlling. They might put less effort and love into the relationship and expect to be loved and cared for without reciprocating.

The partner who is over-giving may feel as if they are losing their sense of self. When we allow another to take from us without reciprocating, we lose our power. We may be easily manipulated and absorb another's feelings of low self-esteem, fears, and unhealed wounds. Still, we often find ourselves trying harder and putting more energy and effort into making the relationship better. If this doesn't work, we may begin to withdraw from our partner in an attempt to gain a better perspective on what is happening. However, once we establish an energy cord connection with another, it is not easy to disconnect. Long after we have ended a relationship, the energy cord remains intact. We might be miles away and have no physical contact with the person and they still may be draining energy from us.

Here are some indications that you have an unhealthy energy cord connection with another:

- You are confused as to why you can't let go and leave a dysfunctional and unhealthy relationship.
- You feel a sense of obligation to be there for another despite feeling unappreciated and unloved by them.

- You give attention, care, and love to another with no reciprocation.
- You put up with treatment that is disrespectful or unloving.
- You never feel like you do or are enough.
- You keep trying and blaming yourself for a relationship that isn't working.
- You obsess or can't stop thinking about another.
- You feel drained, low-energy, and tired, while your partner seems to have more energy.
- You feel controlled by another's thoughts, beliefs, and emotions.
- You find yourself taking on another's mannerisms or opinions.
- You are attracted to unhealthy activities, interests, and behaviors that you previously had no interest in.
- You suddenly crave sugar and carbohydrates or adopt another's food choices and tastes.
- You experience aches and pains that mimic another's physical problems or issues.
- You often dream of someone you had an unhealthy relationship with.
- You feel that you need another's energy to feel good and get anything done.
- Without a partner's energy, you feel exhausted, depressed, and lacking.

It's not always easy to recognize when another person's energy is embedded in our own. While we can transform and heal our difficult emotions, thoughts, and beliefs, we cannot process and transform energy that is not ours. We can only release it. If you find yourself habitually feeling certain emotions such as fear, anger, and grief or you experience physical aches and pains and are unable to process and work through them, you may be absorbing another's energy. Pay attention to the emotions you continually feel that are similar to the predominant emotions of your partner, friends, or family.

For instance, maybe you have a family member who tends to be angry or a partner who is often sad or frustrated. Do you often feel the same feelings that they experience even when you aren't with them? Do you find yourself taking on their opinions, judgments, and viewpoints even though you don't necessarily agree with them? Do you feel depleted, tired, and drained?

If you suspect that you have an energy attachment to another, it is important to release it. Allowing another person to be dependent on your energy and receiving that person's energy will have a detrimental effect on the health and well-being of both of you. The following exercise will assist you in recognizing energy cords and releasing them.

···

EXERCISE
Detaching from Energy Cords

Embedded in our ability to intuit, feel, and sense energy is the capacity to receive and broadcast loving, healing, and transformative frequencies. Get into a relaxed state. Doing this exercise while sitting or lying down in a quiet place is best. Take a long, deep breath, exhaling any stress or tension. Repeat this clearing breath a few times.

Now take a long, deep breath and move the energy of the breath through the body. Tune into the flow of energy through you as you inhale and exhale.

As you continue to focus on the breath, draw your awareness to the top of your head. Take a long, deep inhale, then exhale and move your awareness down through your body. Continue to take relaxing breaths.

As you exhale, scan your physical body and your energy field. When you come to a place of tension or tightness, a knot, or a feeling of emptiness or energy flowing out of you, pause.

Ask yourself, "Is this feeling or sensation due to my energy, or is there an attachment to someone else?"

Don't ask whose energy this is or why you feel it in your body. Too many questions might be confusing and move you out of your intuitive state.

Repeat the question and pause. Continue to take deep breaths and relax.

You will likely feel or get a sense of knowing if the energy you encountered is yours or is from someone else. If you are confused after asking this question and don't get a clear answer, assume that what you are experiencing is a combination of your energy and someone else's.

If this is another person's energy or is a combination of your energy and another's, it needs to be released. Become aware of the area in your body that feels hollow, empty, energetically overactive, or tense. Tune into this area of your body where the cord is attached.

Take a deep breath and become aware of whether it feels as if energy is being drained from you. It may feel as if energy is being pulled or is leaking from a part of your body. It might also feel as if another's energy is entering you.

Sometimes this information will come to you as a sense of knowing rather than a feeling. If you cannot feel a visceral sensation but instead have a sense that energy is draining from you or you are receiving another's energy, trust that this is what is happening.

Imagine that the cord between you and another goes from a part of your body to a part of their body. Energy cords are often attached to the solar plexus, heart, genital area, head, lungs, or hands. However, attachments are possible on any part of the body.

Where does the cord seem to be attached to your partner's body?

Once you get a sense of where you are losing or receiving energy, get a feel for the cord. What is it made of? Does if feel like a steel rod, a silk thread, a mushy glob of energy, a hollow tube, or anything else?

When you are better able to tune into the cord, take whatever action is needed to sever it. You can imagine yourself cutting the cord with scissors or an axe, or maybe you are able to direct a ray of white light onto it to dissolve it. There are innumerable ways to sever the attached cord. If you need help releasing the cord, call upon the force of love or the divine presence to assist you.

You may feel an immediate shift, a sense of relief, or nothing at all. When you request higher support and help, it is present, even if you cannot feel it.

Imagine the force of love as a waterfall of light flowing through you from above your head down to the soles of your feet. Allow your mind, body, heart, and spirit to absorb this cleansing love and healing as it moves through you. Focus on any areas of your physical body or energy field where you sense an energy cord attachment. Fill these places with light, and send the light and love to the person you were attached to.

Imagine that the place in your physical body or energy field that had an attachment is now connected to the force of love through a gold and white wave of light. You now receive waves of high-vibration love.

Imagine that the person from whom you disconnected is also now connected to the light of a higher source.

Once you feel and sense that the detachment process is complete, rest and thank your divine spirit helpers. Write down any insights and feelings that you received while doing this exercise.

As we clear and release our attachments to others, we live in present time. The stuck energy that has kept us bound to another gives way to the pure streams of higher-vibration love energy. As our energy moves back into our being fully and completely, we are able to experience ourselves and reality through a clearer lens. We reclaim our power.

For a few days after this exercise, practice energetic self-care. Avoid crowds, social media, television, and other sources of artificial stimulation for as long as possible. Your energy field is vulnerable and the process of healing may take a few hours or as long as a week or more. Eat well, go for walks in nature, sleep, and open your heart to the force of love.

On some level, the person you detached the cord from is aware that they are no longer connected to you. It is likely that they will try to reestablish the energy cord connection. Be careful. You are vulnerable and may unknowingly allow them to reat-tach. If possible, it is best to avoid contact with the person you detached from until you feel stronger and know why you allowed the attachment to occur. It may take some time to heal and better understand how to love another without creating an unhealthy energetic connection.

Recognize that it is necessary for you to begin to practice a higher expression of love. You serve and bless those you love most effectively when you are centered in the one power of spiritual consciousness and the force of love. While you may be concerned about a loved one, remember that within their heart and spirit the force of love is always present. When we try to be the sole source of love for another and expect them to be that for us, we are out of sync with the true nature of love. As pure as our love for another may be and as much as we may truly love them, we are nurtured and made whole by the force of divine love. When we try to be this love for another, we create unhealthy connections. It is up to each one of us to choose to heal and activate the love within. When we heal ourselves, we create an energetic pattern of healthy self-love that those close to us can follow.

The Love That Heals the Self and Others

How we help others and respond to their needs depends on our level of consciousness. We cannot access levels of energy healing beyond our personal energy frequency and level of consciousness.

When we reside in material consciousness, we are influenced by the power of our external environment and the power that we as individuals possess. We address suffering in others by giving them our time, attention, emotional support, and understanding. While these are positive ways of helping others, if we rely too much on our personal efforts, we become exhausted and depleted. Through material consciousness, our awareness of energy is limited. Because of this, we are prone to unknowingly absorbing the ills, pain, and stress of others and forming energy attachments to them.

Through mental consciousness, we may try to use the power of our mind to eliminate suffering, pain, and imbalance within ourselves and others. We may use healing affirmations and positive thinking and visualize ourselves and others in perfect health and well-being. However, we don't have sufficient power to reverse the influences that exist in the dualism of the material world. We inadvertently reinforce the belief that there is a power that opposes our highest good. The best we can do to help ourselves and others is to attract and increase positive healing energy.

True healing occurs through spiritual consciousness. It is the divine activity within consciousness that transforms suffering. There is no lack, pain, illness, or suffering in the energy of spiritual consciousness. There is only the force of love creating and manifesting our highest good. We don't bring problems and lack into spiritual consciousness and ask that they be healed. Instead, we lift our awareness into the vibration of goodness. This one power cannot be divided and used against itself. It always flows in harmony, creating and manifesting the good through our body, mind, and spirit. We are not using mental tricks and the power of our mind or physical strength and power. Instead, we raise our awareness to the force of love and invite it to flow into every area of our life.

When someone is in the midst of suffering and pain, we can bring them into the flow of spiritual consciousness. When we raise our vibration to this higher frequency, we can invite another's essence and spirit to be present. We don't rely on our personal power alone or take on another's emotions and burdens. Instead, we dwell in the energy of the force of love.

If we focus on another's suffering, we lower our vibration and level of consciousness and compromise our ability to be a conduit for the divine force of love. We don't assume that we know what another needs or will spark their heart to open and heal.

....

EXERCISE
Spiritual Healing

This meditation exercise will empower you to be a conduit of healing and well-being for others. Not only will you not absorb another's energy, but you, too, will experience healing.

Is there someone you know who is in need of help, healing, or relief? This could be someone close to you or even someone you don't know well. It can be a physical, emotional, mental, or spiritual problem or challenge.

Become aware of how you respond emotionally when another is experiencing pain or suffering. Resist absorbing their feelings and overidentifying with what they are experiencing. It is not cold or uncaring of you to not feel what they are feeling. Know that whatever another is experiencing that is causing pain or suffering is a divine opportunity through which they can heal on all levels.

Take a deep, relaxing breath. Get comfortable, close your eyes, and continue to take relaxing breaths. Take long, cleansing inhales and exhale any stress or tension.

Ask within for the force of love to be with you. Continue to breathe cleansing breath and open your heart.

As you breathe and open your heart, become aware of subtle sensations of the force of love. You may experience a warm flow of energy moving through you, a buzzing in your head, or a feeling of expansion. Feel any slight sensations, any tingles of energy, a sense of knowing, or the whispers of a higher presence. Listen within and open your heart.

Take a deep inhale, then exhale and imagine the rich current of love filling your heart and body. As you feel sensations or sense an inner shift and flow of energy moving through you, relax into it.

Breathe and affirm that the divine presence of love manifests in all areas of your life as goodness. The force of love is perfect health, abundance, joy, laughter, love, and all other expressions of the good. Affirm that this goodness is true for you and for all others.

Speak the name of the person with whom you would like to share this higher frequency, and invite them to be a part of this awareness and flow of love. However, it is their choice to accept or to decline if they are not ready.

Imagine an image of the person you are inviting into this love and goodness. Feel the force of love flowing into their being and manifesting as their highest good in every area of their life. Stay with this image and awareness for as long as possible.

Be still and listen within. You are the conduit through which the force of love is flowing out into the world and to those you care for. Feel your love for others and imagine the force of love flowing to all who are in need.

When you feel that this process is complete, affirm that all is well. Your highest good and the good of those you love is manifesting. Every day, make it a practice to open your heart and allow the force of love to be the one power at work in your life.

· ·

The spiritual challenge for empaths, intuitives, and sensitives is to recognize their innate desire to help and heal others. Although we might want to give to, share with, and do all we can for another, it is necessary to create healthy boundaries. Spiritual healing provides an avenue for transformative healing that benefits ourselves and others as well. When we invoke and invite the divine force of love to be the one power at work within our consciousness, healing on some level always takes place. Powerful forces are with you.

CHAPTER 11

Free from Fear

Intuitive and empathic energy protection is a concern for many. As we feel and release our repressed emotions and unhealed wounds and disconnect energy cords, our intuitive and empathic sensing becomes clearer and stronger. This provides us with increased insight and a refined ability to sense and feel the energy vibes of others, the environment, and even spirits. We become empowered to choose the energy that we absorb and connect with. The next step on the path to spiritual consciousness is to make good choices as to the energy we engage with and to more fully understand the protective power of higher frequencies.

Many empaths and the intuitive and sensitive have an innate closeness to the spirit realm. We may feel comforted and watched over and even understood by a presence beyond our five senses. Although we don't always know how or why we trust this intangible something, the connection feels natural. Many receive helpful and insightful guidance, synchronicities, and direction from the unseen forces of love and wisdom. In challenging times or when we are experiencing a loss or deep sadness, we draw comfort from loved ones on the other side, angels, spirit helpers, and the divine presence.

Contact with the spirit realm can be enlightening and transformative, so much so that we might be startled by the intensity and effect it has on us. Even though our conscious connection with loving beings on the other side may last for just a brief moment, the positive effects often stay with us for a long time.

When visitations from the spirit realm occur during troubling or challenging times, they can change the course of our lives. We might become more of a believer in the supernatural, angels, or a higher being. Some feel a renewed sense of purpose and direction and devote their lives to pursuing a specific line of work or vocation. Intuitive abilities get stronger and we continue to experience more clarity and direct messages from the spirit realm. Our desire to continue to evolve and connect with the higher realms is fueled and supported by our contact with the spirit realm.

Ghosts

When we start to experience an increase in our sensitivity to the spirit realm, we are often unsure of what is safe and whether we need to protect ourselves. We may not know if there is something we should or shouldn't be doing to protect ourselves. Unsure of how to proceed, we wonder if we should ignore and avoid these otherworldly interactions or engage. The idea of opening the door to the unknown spirit realm can invoke fear and stress. Some empaths, intuitives, and sensitives have an interest in exploring the presence of ghosts and other manifestations of spirit phenomena. We may want to visit places where there have been unusual happenings, paranormal activity, and sightings of ghosts and spirits.

However, lower-vibration spirits have not ascended into the cleansing and transformative divine state of love and being. They vibrate just a little bit above the material realm. They may inhabit houses or be attached to such things as mirrors and antiques. Some try to get our attention through physical phenomena such as shutting doors, knocking on walls, or mumbled voices. Some spirits who appear as ghosts are lost souls who may not realize that they have passed over. They are confused and are searching and often are attracted to loving and positive people. When we encounter a lost soul spirit, they don't feel threatening or negative. They don't try to invoke fear or make us uncomfortable.

Some lower-vibration spirits that manifest as ghosts have been in a physical body and resisted going into the divine light when they passed over. They may have stubbornly wanted to hold onto worldly things and power. Others don't believe in a divine presence or life after death and are not sure why they still feel that they are alive.

If you become aware of a lost soul or a soul that is holding onto the vibration of the earth realm, you can help them. Say aloud or through a thought message that they no longer belong in the physical realm. Tell them that there is someone or something that is going to come to them from the light and help them move into a better, more loving place.

Don't overly engage with them or ask them questions, as this might lead to them becoming attached to you.

Dark Spirits

Unfortunately, unlike most ghosts, there are dark energy spirits who are intent on inciting fear and are disruptive to those in the physical realm. These misguided spirits may feel more powerful when they provoke, influence, and get a reaction from those in the physical realm. Instead of receiving energy from the divine source, they cling to the dark and want to stay hidden. Fortunately, these dark spirits are rare and have no real power over us.

Low-vibration spirits often send us intuitive information and messages that appeal to our ego. They build us up by being judgmental or critical of others. Boosting our sense of self with false messages, they want us to believe that we are special and better than others. Lower-vibration spirits may try to gain our confidence so they can draw energy from us.

A lot of the messages we receive through spirit beings in the lower vibrations can feel confusing and may contradict previous intuited insights and statements. They may foretell coming misfortune and leave us feeling unsure about or uneasy with the information we receive. In the presence of a dark spirit, we may be nauseous, our skin may feel clammy, or we may feel tired or hopeless or think that we are more powerful and worthy than others.

If you get a sense that there is something present that isn't good for you, trust your intuition. Although you may have felt comforted during past encounters with the spirit realm, this is not always the case. We are most vulnerable to attracting and connecting with lower-vibration spirits when we are under the influence of drugs or alcohol or when we are unconscious for any length of time. If we are perpetually angry, negative, or mean-spirited or have thoughts of hurting or taking advantage of others, we are more susceptible to their influence. Under normal circumstances, we aren't at risk of attracting dark spirits. We have dominion over our physical being and cannot be intruded upon by the unseen without our consent.

Intuitive Warnings

One of the ways our intuition seeks to care for us is by operating as a primal warning system. For instance, have you ever felt nervous or edgy in the presence of another for no known reason? Have you ever wanted to flee a situation or get away from someone and not know why? Perhaps you've immediately felt a twinge of uncomfortableness or fear when first meeting someone. When another's energy feels confusing or negative despite the fact that they appear to be harmless, do you listen to your intuition?

When we are in a potentially dangerous or unhealthy situation or with those with bad intentions, our intuitive and empathic ability tries to alert us. Even though someone or something may not appear to be problematic or harmful, pay attention to your intuition and the vibes you feel and receive. All too often we ignore and disregard empathic and intuitive warning signals because outer appearances give us no rational reason for worry or alarm. Trust your intuitive and empathic impressions and gut feelings. This is often your most accurate early warning system. Even when you don't have evidence or a rational understanding of what you receive, trust yourself.

Intuitive messages of potential danger usually show up as stress and tension in the body. Gut feelings, tightness in the throat or chest, a fight-or-flight response, and a feeling of heightened watchfulness and anxiousness are common intuitive warnings of danger. Sometimes being blocked or prevented from doing something or going somewhere is a form of protection. Missing flights, arriving late, forgetting plans, getting stuck in traffic, or losing car keys may be ways to keep you safe from making a mistake.

Sometimes our intuitive warning system shows up through increased awareness, sensitivity, and sensations. For instance, years ago, I opened the door to enter a restaurant and it felt like I hit a brick wall. There was a visceral feeling that an external force was stopping me from going forward. The feeling was strong, undeniable, and unexpected. I couldn't think of any reason why I shouldn't go into this particular restaurant and eat, yet I knew that I was being given a warning and didn't go in. I never understood why this happened, but I know that I did the right thing.

Trust your gut feelings even if you have no tangible evidence. Walk away when something doesn't feel right. You don't have to explain your actions or feelings to anyone, and don't let anyone talk you out of what you intuitively feel.

Repressed Emotions versus Intuiting Danger

When our repressed emotions and unhealed wounds are suddenly triggered and surface, it may feel as if our intuition is alerting us to danger. Intuitive vibes such as the hair on our arms standing up, a sudden stomachache, feelings of anxiety or panic, or the feeling that something is off or amiss can be a warning. It is also possible that something in our environment is triggering our stuffed-down emotions or unhealed wounds.

Continually experiencing similar intuitive feelings and vibes in different situations and with different people is likely due to stuffed-down unresolved emotions or unhealed wounds. If you feel that you often intuit the stress, fear, or anxiety of others, this might be a message from your inner self that something within you is out of balance and in need of healing. If you frequently have trust issues with others or fear their hidden motives, this might indicate unresolved issues from past relationships.

Our intuition always acts in our best interest. The uncomfortable feelings and sensations that we may feel aren't meant to be confusing or cause us pain or stress. Our body, mind, and spirit are always moving us into deeper levels of healing and well-being. When we listen within and pay attention to our intuitive sensations and feelings, we can gain valuable insight into what within us needs our attention.

For instance, maybe your father was perpetually angry and moody and often found fault with you. He projected his discontent onto you, and everyone in the family treated this as normal. Your mother and other family members never came to your defense or confronted him about his behavior. It was *just how Dad was*. Now, as an adult, you question the motives of men who are attracted to you. Although there is no abuse or disrespect in your current relationship, you feel that your intuition is telling you that you can't trust your boyfriend. The slightest hint that he might not be who he seems to be makes you continually defensive.

However, this isn't what is happening. Your intuition isn't trying to warn you. Instead, your inner knowing is attempting to draw your attention to the repressed feelings and wounds from childhood that are keeping you from creating a loving relationship. Because of the past unhealed and unacknowledged wounds that your father inflicted on you, you feel that the problem lies with your potentially abusive boyfriend. Once you become aware that the intuitive feelings of mistrust and defensiveness are coming from within, you can further explore and pursue your own healing.

Psychic Protection Techniques

Many empaths, intuitives, and sensitives have a tendency to absorb and feel the negativity and toxic emotions and thoughts of others. We may also be concerned that we might attract a dark or low-vibration spirit or presence. Feelings of trepidation and the fear of unseen powers and the spirit world have been with us since the beginning of time. When we can't see, hear, or touch something with our five senses, many will dismiss its existence or become wary and nervous.

Our fear of being influenced and affected by the energy of others or dark spirits depends in part on our level of consciousness. Through a solely material understanding and consciousness, the belief that we can absorb and feel another's emotions and thoughts is too abstract an idea to accept. The notion of intuitive and empathic abilities and sensitivity is often viewed as a weakness.

Although material consciousness might not fully accept the validity of intuitive and empathic awareness, there is a belief in the forces of good and evil. Spirits not only exist, but are up to no good and can cause potential harm. We must guard and protect ourselves from the unseen realm of spirits and other beings. We may seek the protection of a higher power by doing our best to be moral, honest, and good. Otherwise, we fear that we may inadvertently open ourselves to the influence of dark forces.

Through material consciousness, we might also understand the value of using crystals, flower essences, and herbs to repel low-vibration spirits and dark energy. Using the smoke of bundled dried sage and other herbs is a common way to remove unwanted energy. Clearing a space of dark energy entails burning the bundle of herbs until it emits a thick smoke, then moving slowly through a room, house, car, or other area and allowing the smoke to gather. If it feels like there is negative energy or there are unwanted spirits in your home or office or surrounding you, the smoke of dried herbs can eliminate these influences.

Although there are those who view life through the lens of material consciousness, many have evolved into a more mental understanding and embrace the power of the mind. When we begin to recognize that we are more than a physical being, our soul and spirit energy becomes more tangible and real. While material consciousness perceives power as external and outside of the self, mental consciousness embraces our inner power. We no longer look outside of ourselves for solutions and answers. This helps us be better equipped to explore possibilities and generate ideas through which we can keep ourselves safe from the energy of others and the unseen realm.

Through mental consciousness, the power of the mind and positive thought is often utilized for psychic protection. Our words are messengers that call to us or repel varying levels of energy vibration. Words release our intent out into the creative universe.

Through mental consciousness, we welcome the positive and higher vibrations while avoiding individuals and situations that we feel have negative, low vibrations.

The power of white light is also often invoked for protection from negativity and possible dark energies and beings. White-light energy embodies the purest and highest form of divine energy and acts as a shield that protects us from low-vibration and harmful energy. White light has no opposition and cannot be influenced or affected by negative or dark energy. Low and dense vibrations cannot affect or penetrate the higher realms of light. When we ask for the protection of white light and imagine it surrounding us, the dark has no power. White light acts as a protective energetic coating that repels lower energies. It's kind of like wearing cosmic rain gear that repels negativity and toxicity and keeps us safe and warm.

Affirmations are focused statements that attract and manifest our desires into being. To invoke psychic protection, positive affirmations and white-light energy are often used together.

Here are some examples of mental consciousness protection affirmations:

- I am surrounded and protected by white light.
- I attract only positive and loving energy.
- I receive only what is in my highest good.

When repeatedly spoken, positive, affirming statements strengthen our mind and heart and align us with high-vibration energy.

Although these types of protection are powerful, they have limitations. We don't always remember or recognize when we need to invoke and surround ourselves with white light. Empaths and the intuitive and sensitive often have the ability to feel the goodness and love in others, even when people don't see it within themselves. This can lead to trusting someone who may be potentially harmful to us. We might forget or not feel the need to protect ourselves when we are in the company of those we feel need understanding and help. Even when others are acting in less than loving ways, we might underestimate the effect that their energy can have on us.

Another concern is our susceptibility to absorbing energy randomly and without always knowing that we are doing so. We intuit and absorb the energy not just of those we know, but of those we don't know as well. Going to a conference, being on a plane, or riding in an elevator might not seem to be an energetic risk. However, if we are exhausted, ill, or having a challenging day, we are especially sensitive and vulnerable to absorbing the energy of others and the environment. As we go about our day-to-day lives, we don't always feel the need or remember to protect ourselves. We may inadvertently absorb negativity and other lower-vibration emotions and thoughts without realizing it.

For these and other reasons, invoking protection is not a foolproof protection strategy. We are borrowing higher-vibration energy, not generating it. There is a better and more effective way to repel and stop absorbing toxic, negative, and unwanted energy from others and the environment.

Where Darkness Cannot Penetrate

Spiritual consciousness makes a radical shift away from the fear of negativity and dark energy and the power of another's emotions and thoughts to adversely affect us. Through spiritual consciousness, there is nothing to protect ourselves from. There is only one power, and this power is creative, high-vibration divine source energy. Spiritual consciousness is more than a perspective or an understanding; it is a transmutation into a higher state of being. In moments when we connect with spiritual consciousness, we are no longer subject to the material laws of duality and limitation. Spiritual consciousness is the ascension into the divine source where there is no fear or resistance to the good.

We don't have to be highly evolved and perfect to experience and embody spiritual consciousness. Many feel they are not good enough to attain this higher level of awareness. Our mistakes, poor choices, and misguided attempts to love and receive love may lead us to believe that we are unworthy. We may feel that we are more likely to experience negativity and the sorrow and heavy feelings of others than we are the light of an unbounded and deep love.

Spiritual consciousness is an aspect of who we are and our eternal being. Although we aren't usually aware of it, the power of the divine is within us. As we feel and free ourselves from our repressed emotions and unhealed wounds, we allow the force of love to fill our mind, heart, body, and soul. Empaths and the intuitive and sensitive have an aptitude for recognizing energy. This empowers us to feel the higher vibrations and align with spiritual consciousness. As the force of love moves into our awareness, our perception of ourselves and the world as we know it transforms. We are lifted beyond the reach of dark energies and lower-vibration emotions and feelings such as fear and negativity. The grip that another's energy has had on us loosens. We no longer absorb the toxic and unhealthy vibes from which we believed there was no escape. We don't need to shield ourselves, as there is nothing to protect ourselves from in spiritual consciousness. Dark spirits flee from the light of spiritual consciousness, because they are aware that in the light, they no longer exist. They have no power and dissolve into nothingness, like mist in the sun.

Through our intuitive and empathic sensitivity, we still feel and sense the full range of human emotions and feelings. However, the lower vibrations of energy such as negativity, fear, and anger don't attach and stick to us. Through inner whispers and knowing, we are alerted to the people and situations that may cause us harm or not be in our highest good. Through the clarity of spiritual consciousness, we more quickly sense and feel another's ill intent and can avoid potential problems and naturally steer clear of unsafe situations.

....

EXERCISE
The Inner Refuge

If you become nervous or fear that you are absorbing negativity or that there is a lower-vibration energy or a dark spirit present, remind yourself that there is only one power. Breathe and don't dwell on the fear of what could happen.

Take some long, deep, relaxing breaths, exhaling any stress or tension. Become aware that in the presence of the divine, there can be no darkness or evil. Spiritual consciousness has no opposition, and there is nothing that can influence or affect it. It is always operating in your highest good.

Breathe white light down through the top of your head and move it through your body. Continue to breathe in cleansing white light and exhale any stress, tension, or fear. Feel the force of love as it expands within your heart, mind, and body.

As you breathe, allow divine white light to surround and envelop you.

As you continue to breathe, listen within for the quiet whispers of divine presence. Let it speak to you of its power, presence, and protection. It might sound something like this:

I am with you. You are loved, cared for, and watched over. There is no external or internal force that can enter into the sacred space of your being. The light within cannot falter or be extinguished. There can be no separation between who you are and the light that I am.

Feel the light grow stronger within you. Breathe into your heart and soul, and let it assure you of its never-ending love and presence.

Continue to breathe and allow white light to flow through your being.
....

Whenever you feel a need for protection, use this prayer:

Prayer of Protection

May the flow of the divine force of love be within me
and surrounding me.
All darkness disperses and evaporates.
In this high-frequency light, only the good can draw near.
All else falls away into the nothingness that it is.
I am safe.

The spiritual challenge is to recognize when we are intuiting uncomfortable, negative, or toxic energy and not react with fear and avoidance. Instead, we can use the awareness that there may be a lower-vibration spirit or negative and toxic energy present to draw close to the white light of protection and shift into the awareness of the one power of spiritual consciousness.

PART IV
Allowing the Good

CHAPTER 12

Surrendering and Allowing

Through spiritual consciousness, we do without doing anything at all and our highest good flows to us. As we let go of our reliance on our ego's need to control and dominate, we strengthen our trust and awareness of our spirit. Through surrendering and allowing, this next step moves us deeper into alignment with divine presence.

Everything in nature surrenders and works in unison with a silent wisdom. Leaves fall to the ground, surrendering to the cold and wind in the autumn. Seeds scatter in the dirt, allowing the sun and rain to break them open. The clouds gather and release the moisture that has filled them. The moon, seas, butterflies, and green sprouts emerging from the dark soil don't overthink their purpose or worry about anything. All of nature follows the dictates of an invisible and masterful wisdom.

We humans have lost our ability to perceive and respond to a greater knowing that guides all of creation. The noise and drama of the material world demands our attention. Our needs and fears and the day-to-day slew of problems and concerns we encounter direct our attention to worldly answers. Letting go and surrendering to something that feels intangible and unknowable hardly feels like a solution. Yet when our thinking mind is still and we suspend the belief that we must figure it all out, guiding inner whispers are present.

Feeling and releasing the stuffed-away emotions, unhealed wounds, and energy cords allows the current of the force of love to move freely through our being. However, we don't always hear and trust the gentle whispers of divine presence. While we may sense, feel, and have moments of connection with the force of love, it may seem elusive and hard to grasp. Through material and mental consciousness, aligning with high-frequency divine activity may seem impractical and without benefit. Our everyday life concerns, problems, and issues seem to demand a more practical approach and material remedies. We may feel that trusting an illusive presence and power may be fine for a monk living in a monastery but not for us. When we are focused on the power of the material world, the idea of spiritual energy might not seem to offer much in return.

Material, mental, and spiritual consciousness are all within us. Our multidimensional nature allows us to continually experience reality through these different perspectives. While power appeals to our ego through the lens of material and mental consciousness, power through spiritual consciousness is centered in our heart and spirit essence. While our varied levels of consciousness are all a part of us, we use them to interpret who we are and the world around us differently. It is the inner voice that we listen to and what we focus our awareness on that determine what we experience and manifest.

The transition into spiritual consciousness is a process where we are continually faced with the choice of believing in worldly or spiritual power. Worldly power is based in the belief that there is limited abundance and we must compete with others to be more deserving and reap the benefits. Those who have less are destined to struggle forever for their small share. There is no compassion or support in worldly power. It yields an unjust sword and takes down those who are weak, different, and outside of the norm. We have come to believe that power is a dominating force that can push us to the top of the heap or bury us with uncaring scorn. The fear that what we have could be lost or taken from us by such things as a downturn in the economy or ill health or through our personal failings creates constant stress.

Through material and mental consciousness, our default is to believe that we must solve, handle, and tackle whatever comes our way. When we depend on our personal efforts alone, we continue to feel powerless and at odds with a demanding world. It is up to us to make things right, find solutions, keep the ball rolling, and manage the challenges we confront. When we hold onto the belief that we know what is in our best interest and how to go about getting it, we block divine creative activity.

We have been programmed to believe that spiritual consciousness deals exclusively with our spiritual needs and aspirations. It is centered in the unknown and the beyond, not in our daily concerns. We may pray for better times, for healing and abundance, but we don't know if they will come our way or not. However, the ways of the divine are not empty and ineffective in the physical world.

Spiritual consciousness is a radical departure from the belief that the good comes into our lives through struggle, luck, talent, and mental strength. It is not solely through our personal efforts and fortunate external influences that our needs, wants, and desires are met. Instead, when we surrender and allow the force of love to move into our being, we are lifted beyond the limited laws of the material and mental realms. The never-ending abundance of divine creativity is the active principle of our consciousness. As we surrender our everyday concerns, worries, and desires to the natural rhythm and flow of the wise and loving divine presence, the powerful current of goodness and abundance manifests.

Beyond Cause and Effect

Through spiritual consciousness, divine creative activity seeps into and interrupts the finite limitations of the material world that is governed by cause and effect and duality. Through the material law of cause and effect, we eventually encounter all that we set in motion. Our good comes to us as a result of our actions, thoughts, feelings, and activity. If we make a mistake, get angry, or think a negative thought, it will come back to us and manifest in some form. To know why we are manifesting certain experiences, we look to our past actions, thoughts, and attitude. To know what will manifest in the future, we look to our thoughts, emotions, and what we are putting into action in the present. The law of cause and effect can be used to better our lives and create more happiness. This is one of the basic principles of mental consciousness. Positive thinking and affirmations are ways to put into motion the power of our thoughts to create our desires.

However, material and mental consciousness operate under the constraints of duality. As much effort as we put into consciously creating through the power of our mind and through our actions, we are always up against the opposite. Thinking positive thoughts gives power to the negative, what is unwanted follows what is wanted, challenges give way to ease, and disappointment follows happiness. Despite the efforts we put into creating our good through cause and effect, the cycles of opposing forces continue endlessly.

Until we ascend into spiritual consciousness, there is no escape from these patterns. The one power of divine presence has no opposition and is not influenced by what we have done in the past, the mistakes we have made, and the wrongs we have committed. When divine creative activity is at work within our consciousness, we are no longer bound to our past actions, missteps, and mistakes.

Spiritual consciousness offers us a path out of the never-ending cycle of cause and effect. Instead of judging what we experience, we understand it as a lesson and stepping stone for our advancement. The force of love is within all things, people, situations, and experiences. We can never fully know and judge the significance of what is happening in our life and the lives of others. Whatever we are experiencing becomes the gateway for the highest good to manifest, even if this doesn't seem possible.

No matter what we are experiencing in the material realm, the shift into spiritual consciousness can occur through unexpected events, changes, and upheavals. Divine creative activity is not dependent on the things of this world. It is always creating new possibilities and manifesting as the good, even when appearances suggest otherwise.

The force of love doesn't judge or discriminate. Most of us try to do the right and good thing in any given situation and may feel disappointment or guilt when we fail. We look to what others and our community and culture define as good and bad to help us make our choices and guide our behavior.

We can surrender everything to the force of love, which doesn't respond to our past actions and choices, even if we haven't always done what we consider to be the right thing. Despite our flaws, the force of love is always present and acts with each one of us exactly the same. It is not selective and doesn't pick who to help and who to deny.

We move out of duality and cause and effect when we surrender our issues, problems, wants, and needs to the divine presence. To become more comfortable with letting go of your worries and concerns, become aware of your responses to everyday stresses and pressures. When confronted with challenging situations, thoughts, emotions, or experiences, pay attention to your automatic perception and reaction. Instead of responding with stress and anxiety or feeling victimized, recognize that you have a choice. Pause and release your stress and worries into the divine presence.

It can be especially difficult to let go and surrender issues that have importance and affect us personally. Even though our expectations of what should happen and our desire for a certain outcome appear to be based in sound judgment, they come from the finite, limited part of us. We are like a sailboat that maps its journey across the vast ocean based on how it navigates in a small pond. Our vision is restricted and our understanding limited. We just can't see the full picture or all of the possibilities. Even when we think we do, we aren't able to fully perceive and understand what is in our highest good and the highest good of others. While we all want abundance, joy, love, and positive relationships, the path through which these arrive is often a divine mystery.

It is often those who suffer, the ill and the lost and lonely, who have an easier time relinquishing control to a higher presence. This isn't because they have been chosen for special blessings. Instead, it is in times of suffering that we recognize our limitations and are able to surrender to a greater power and presence. We find the courage to allow our good to manifest. When we have nothing and no hope in our ability to get our needs met, we are more likely to accept spiritual help. We don't always think about supernatural assistance when we experience success, afflu-ence, and admiration from others.

As we leave behind the outer and inner voices pushing us to manage our issues through the force of our will, we enter into the quiet and stillness of the force of love. This is the calm in the midst of outer chaos and disruption, love and comfort when there is grief and understanding, and clarity when confronting confusion. It is the bridge that connects us to the deep rhythms of the universe and the silent whisper that reverberates through our soul, waking us to the greater good.

The following meditation provides a blueprint for surrender. It can be helpful to focus on a challenging area of your life or a nagging issue and practice releasing it. Surrender isn't a one-time experience and event. Throughout the day, make it a practice to let go of control and trust in the force of love that is always pres-ent. Whether it is a general feeling of dissatisfaction, a specific issue or challenge you are confronting, or something you would like to manifest, open and allow the divine presence to create your good.

··

MEDITATION
Letting Go to the Force of Love

Become comfortable and begin to take long, deep, relax-ing breaths. Exhale any stress and tension. Continue to breathe and release any stress and anxiety through the exhale. Breathe and relax.

Begin by calling to mind the issue, concern, need, or desire that you would like to release to a higher presence. Silently within your heart or aloud, say something like this:

*I release and let go of _____ (insert concern or worry)
to the force of love.*

You can repeat this statement a few times while you
take a deep, long inhale, exhale, and relax. As you continue to take deep breaths, become aware of any stress,
anxiety, worry, fear, or grief. You can place your hand on
the area of your body where it feels like stress, anxiety,
tension, or pain is the most intense.

Repeat the phrase:

*I release and let go of _____ (insert concern or worry)
to the force of love.*

*Even though I don't always trust what may happen and
it's hard not to step in and try to control the outcome, my
intention is to allow divine presence to intervene for my
highest good.*

Continue to breathe and let go.

For some, it may be helpful to imagine the force of love
as a flowing white ribbon of light absorbing your stress,
concerns, and worries.

Become aware of any inner shifts and sensations. Listen for the still, soft whispers of the divine presence, a
quivering in your heart and soul, and the inner assurance
that divine activity is at work in your life.

As you continue to focus your attention inward, listen,
feel, and become aware of any sensations, messages, and
insights. Let go of your expectations of how and when
your highest good will manifest. Surrendering your need
to be in control allows the divine to be the activity at work
within your consciousness. Allow your concerns, prob-

lems, and challenges to be transported beyond the limitations of cause and effect. Breathe and open your heart and fill yourself with the higher divine frequencies.

You may want to write down any inner guidance or direction you receive during this exercise.

Pay attention to your intuition, inner guidance, and dreams and be alert for synchronicities for the next few days, weeks, or even months. In some form, divine activity will manifest as your highest good.

Repeat this practice as many times as you feel is necessary and are led to do. Each time, let go and surrender more fully and completely. As we practice consciously releasing and letting go of our worries, stresses, concerns, and control, the force of love intervenes. What manifests is always greater and more satisfying than what we are able to give to ourselves. Divine love manifests in whatever form is most aligned with our highest good. This might come as an increase in finances, career opportunities, physical or emotional healing or relief from pain, insights that bring understanding, relationship harmony, and all forms of abundance.

Notice the moments when you suspect that a greater presence is at work in your life. Be thankful for the peace, well-being, comfort, and increases that come your way. When you experience anything good in your life, don't try to hold onto it or overthink. Receive it fully without thought, and let it be. Have gratitude for the small ways that you are being taken care of and watched over. The more we appreciate the good and allow it to show up, the more we receive.

Loving Ourselves

The force of love flows freely, like a warm and gentle spring breeze spreading seeds of new life. It doesn't pick and choose where to blossom, yet it is up to us to become the rich, fertile soil where it takes root. Our highest good shows up where we surrender and allow it to. Divine presence often has a light step that we are not always aware of. It doesn't arrive with grand gestures or expect loud applause. The force of love is easily missed. It's not always obvious that it is divine presence bringing us ease in the midst of struggle, abundance during times of lack, and healing and help when we feel no hope. While the force of love doesn't stand on stage and announce our special status, it does free us to receive our highest good. It is from the back of the room, in the small acts of letting go and allowing, that our good emerges.

Letting go and surrendering to a higher presence and power doesn't come naturally. As we surrender and invite divine creative activity to be our center of power, we integrate spiritual consciousness into our everyday experience. Releasing our stuffed-away emotions and unhealed wounds clears the way for the force of love to flow through us more fully. It is through loving ourselves that we fully activate the force of love and integrate it into every area of our life. Loving ourselves is the channel through which we allow our good to arrive.

Self-love has a multitude of aspects and expressions. It may be setting boundaries with others who would take advantage of us and don't perceive our self-worth. Taking care of ourselves is listening to, trusting, and acting on our truth. Withdrawing from negativity and outer chaos and the demands of others is an expression of self-love. Loving ourselves is taking time to rest and not engaging with people who try to rob us of our serenity and in activities that drain our inner reserves.

Be kind and compassionate to yourself when fears, negative self-talk, judgmental attitudes, and criticisms surface. Notice the constant inner dialogue of the chattering voice and don't argue with it, ignore it, or try to convince it of anything. Instead of focusing on the chattering mind, become aware of the unyielding generosity of divine love. No further from us than our breath and the beating of our heart, the force of love is always present. Love yourself with this soothing, nonjudgmental, and calming presence. Remind yourself that there is only one power at work in your life, and it always flows in the direction of goodness.

These kinds of statements reinforce and remind us to love ourselves:

- I love myself through challenges and difficulties and release my stress to the force of love.

- Things don't always go the way I expect them to, and that's okay. My highest good may look different from what I thought it would.

- I don't have the power to control and change the nature of the material realm. However, it doesn't have the power to control my destiny.

- There is an infinite supply of abundance, love, and goodness that is always present. I allow myself to receive it.

Practicing self-love in our day-to-day lives aligns us with the force of love. As we rise to this higher frequency, divine creative activity manifests through us. Love all of who you are, even the parts of yourself that are trapped in the low vibrations of emotions such as self-blame, resentment, anger, and guilt. Surrender these emotions to the divine presence, and they will be transformed. Despite our level of consciousness, loving ourselves is a catalyst through which we ascend into higher aspects of self.

We are known, seen, and loved not just in this life, but eternally. We have journeyed through many lifetimes, experiencing all manner of challenges and difficulties. Many on a spiritual path have chosen a life plan that entails some degree of suffering. We don't do this to punish ourselves, and we are not victims of chance and unfortunate circumstance. Everything we encounter is an invitation to open our heart. Don't judge what you are experiencing or encounter. Accept it all as stepping stones to higher awareness. Invite the uncertainty, misunderstandings, and frustrations into your heart without resistance. Instead of focusing on why something has occurred, ask what it has to teach you. Love yourself without reservation through the pain and confusion that comes to your door. Imagine those you love dearly and without reservation, such as a child, partner, spouse, or friend. Love yourself in the way you love them.

....

EXERCISE
Loving Ourselves

Loving ourselves opens and allows us to receive. Although we may want a higher divine presence to manifest through us, the idea of opening our heart, mind, and being to an invisible force is an abstract idea for many. It can feel a bit scary and foolish to open and let go and allow something that we cannot name or fully know to move through us. We are not accustomed to putting our trust in anything other than our personal efforts and tangible resources. We may not know how to surrender and allow. It is when the ego's chattering voice of ridicule, doubt, stress, and fear is present that we most need to allow the higher love of spiritual consciousness to be present. When we love ourselves through difficult and challenging feelings, we allow divine healing to flow through us.

This exercise will help you release any inner resistance to loving yourself and allowing the higher forces of love to love you too.

To begin, relax and breathe and become aware of at least five times when you acted in unloving ways toward yourself.

It is not always obvious when we act in unkind and unloving ways, such as engaging in negative self-talk, having too high of expectations, not taking care of our health, overworking, not listening within to our needs, dismissing our uncomfortable feelings, or feeling undeserving and unworthy.

As you become aware of at least five unloving acts or behaviors, write them down.

Focus on the first unloving act or behavior. Say aloud or within:

I surrender the unloving behavior of _____ (insert the action or behavior) to the force of love.

Place your hand on your heart and repeat this statement until you feel that you are truly ready to let go of the pain that prompted this behavior. Feel the pain you caused yourself. Let go and surrender whatever known or unknown energy is preventing you from feeling the higher vibrations of love. Breathe and imagine that you are surrendering your wounds, fears, and protective shields into the flow of the force of love. As you release the heaviness of your heart, it dissipates and is transformed. Continue to breathe, open your heart, and let go and release.

When you feel a release and letting go, move on to the next statement.

Continue this process until you have surrendered all of the unloving examples and any other ones that may have surfaced while doing the exercise.

Now imagine a time when you felt truly loved. Maybe this love came from another person, a pet, or a child, or perhaps your heart filled with love unexpectedly while in the beauty of nature or in a quiet moment. Open your heart and feel the warmth and assurance of love.

Think of five or more actions that you can take to truly love yourself and write them down.

Focus on the first behavior or act of self-love that you wrote down and place your hand on your heart. Say aloud or within:

I commit to loving myself by _____ (insert the act or behavior or self love).

Continue in this way until you have committed to each statement of self-love.

Once you have completed this, imagine a luminous, vibrating force of love more powerful than any love that you have ever felt in the past. Ask within if there is any restriction or block that is preventing you from receiving and filling your heart with this love.

Be patient and listen within. A memory may surface, or perhaps a feeling or sensation of tightness, or you may feel a protective wall surrounding your heart. Imagine that you are releasing whatever surfaces to the force of love.

Once you feel clear, take a long, deep breath and allow the luminous light of love into your heart, mind, and being. Breathe into your heart and notice the subtle shifts of the force of love. A tingle of energy may move up your spine or the warm flow of love may fill your heart. You may feel your awareness expand as a gentle inner humming or vibration moves through you. Deeper relaxation, the release of tension, and the unwinding of tightness and stress may occur. Give way to the inner sensations. You may feel the subtle presence of comfort and warmth. Listen within for the quiet whispers of spirit, and invite any insights and sensations into your awareness. Feel the gentle nudges and whispers of the divine presence in your heart. Throughout the day, listen within to the presence of spirit and allow your good to emerge.

Through spiritual consciousness, our stress unwinds and the grip that our inner pain and suffering have had on us softens. While we still may worry at times and get wrapped up in our daily concerns and unloving behaviors, the inner awareness that there is another way exerts a stronger influence. Instead of our addictive habit of believing that we are powerless and blaming ourselves and others for what we are experiencing, we surrender to a greater force. Loving ourselves and accepting all that comes our way allows us to fully receive the manifestations of divine love.

The spiritual challenge is to let go of control and surrender our concerns, problems, expectations, and anxiety to the flow of the force of love. As long as we attempt to control outcomes and rely on our personal efforts alone, our ego directs our path. Spiritual consciousness operates outside of the laws of material cause and effect. The good doesn't come to us because we are more deserving than others and it doesn't pass us by because of our mistakes. Instead, it flows into our life through our readiness and willingness to let go and receive it. When we no longer believe and act on everything that our chattering mind tells us is true and instead trust the still, small whispers of the divine within, we are surrendering to a higher presence and power. Practice this kind of surrender with the big and small issues, stresses, and challenges. As we let go of the belief that it is only through our personal efforts that our good comes to us, we integrate divine creative activity into our consciousness and ascend out of the mundane and into the extraordinary.

CHAPTER 13

Manifest with Ease

The divine is always present within our heart, mind, body, and spirit. It is in the inner silence that we make conscious contact with it and receive the higher divine frequencies needed for manifestation. As the divine becomes the activity within our consciousness, all things align with our highest good. Releasing and clearing out our stuffed-away emotions, unhealed wounds, and unhealthy energy cords creates the space for the light to enter.

This next step strengthens our innermost communion with the gentle whispers of the force of love. This transcendent journey is not linear, and there is no end and no beginning. It is more of a spiral through which we continually evolve into higher frequencies. As we listen within and allow divine vibrations to integrate throughout our mind, body, and spirit, we are guided step-by-step into an unfolding way of life that allows for true freedom and joy.

Our challenge is to attune our intuitive and empathic sensitivity to the inner quiet and rest in this peace. We are constantly pulled into the energy web of the world and the thoughts and feelings of others. The constant hum of outer activity seems to

drown out the inner silence, where we can encounter the whispers of divine presence. Such things as cell phones, computers,
and social media notifications constantly vie for our attention.
If we don't respond to emails and text messages immediately, we
may seem rude or others might begin to worry about us. While
we may be aware that the continual noise in our life often causes
us stress and exhaustion, it doesn't always seem possible to opt
out. Even for those involved in spirituality and mind-body-spirit
awareness, there is the expectation that we will interact, respond,
and keep up.

If our empathic, intuitive, and sensitive nature is overly focused
on the material world, we tend to unknowingly feel and absorb the
emotions, attitudes, and consciousness of those in our environment. When we are energetically tangled up in worldly conditions,
we become enmeshed in the vast spectrum of chaotic energy. The
way of the world is duality, and it will always be a roller coaster of
ups and downs, good and bad, positive and negative, and happiness and suffering. Within the worldly paradigm of duality, it can
be no other way.

Our empathic, intuitive, and sensitive channels aren't meant
to be taking in and absorbing unpredictable and often toxic and
low-vibration energy. While what we intuitively feel and receive
may be accurate, it is not necessarily helpful, wise, and loving.
Instead, feeling another's emotions, tuning into their thoughts,
and sensing the energy of an environment may feel heavy and be
stress-inducing. There is little trustworthy and helpful guidance
in the material realm. However, this is where our intuitive and
empathic sensitivities are often focused.

Even though we often are not conscious of our connection to
the divine, we are never separate and apart from it. The force of
love is alive within us, and we are part of the whole of creation.

We exist simultaneously in the physical and spiritual realms and the seen and unseen. Over time we have dulled and forgotten our innate ability to commune with the source of all creation.

The root of our allegiance to the power of the material world and the devaluing of the spirit realm is embedded in our collective consciousness. For centuries we have been influenced by a pervasive conditioning that is fueled by the fear, greed, and thirst for power of material consciousness. We have been led to believe that we must play by the rules of those in positions of authority and worldly power in order to meet our basic needs and thrive. Over time, cultural, political, and societal norms and institutions have become the dominant influence shaping our views and beliefs.

As we better understand the pervasive conditioning that the material realm yields in our mind and heart, we become better able to release its hold on us. Throughout the day, notice the issues and challenges you confront and pay attention to your unconscious assumptions and judgments. As you become aware of your deep-seated biases, beliefs, and assumptions, your shift into spiritual consciousness progresses.

Contemplate these questions and statements:

- Do I believe that the spiritual realm is far removed from my material and physical concerns?
- Do I feel that it is only through my personal efforts that I overcome challenges and difficulties?
- Do I really believe that I can surrender and receive the things in my life that are in my highest good?
- When I listen within, I don't feel or hear anything. There is nothing there for me.

- I'm not good at meditating and becoming inwardly quiet. I'll never be able to connect with the force of love or divine presence.
- If I can't receive a clear and direct intuitive message, I must be doing something wrong.
- Can I surrender and trust that there is a force that is manifesting my good through me?
- I need something more tangible than spiritual energy to rely on and trust.
- Can I receive what is in my highest good without self-sabotage and resistance?

You likely identify with several of these questions and statements. This doesn't mean that the divine presence isn't with you and working through you to manifest your highest good. There is no standard of perfection that you have to achieve or a right way to shift into spiritual consciousness. Your connection with divine presence is personal to you. Your ego isn't familiar with your spirit or higher-frequency energy and will argue against this invisible presence. The belief that you must be able to meditate and connect to and hear the divine in a certain way is coming from the ego.

Surrender your resistance and inability to be inwardly quiet, to hear messages, and to fully let go of your worries and concerns. Surrender the worn-out thoughts and emotions that appear to be more powerful than your desire to shift into a new way of being. Surrender any known or unknown beliefs and assumptions that may be hindering your ability to fully open to and allow the divine force of love to be the power within you.

Through spiritual consciousness, we can activate a more powerful presence. Conscious contact with divine energy shifts us out of the grip of the material world. Pure divine creative energy is endlessly manifesting, without any worry or stress on our part. We can simply surrender to and flow with the force of love. Letting go into this powerful current sets in motion the infusion of higher frequencies within our heart, mind, and body. There is nothing we encounter in the material realm that can oppose this state of divine creative activity.

It is not always easy for us to shift from material and mental consciousness into spiritual awareness, but this is what we are called to do. The more often we make the choice to move our awareness out of the beliefs, limitations, and programmed responses of the material and mental realms, the more natural and effortless it becomes. The following exercise can be helpful in transitioning into spiritual consciousness.

....

MEDITATION
Shifting into Spiritual Consciousness

There will be times, likely often, when there are many voices within you vying for your attention. Worries, concerns, stresses, and problems plague you. As much as you would like to settle into a peaceful meditation, it is not possible. Instead of giving up and dissolving into a stressful state, sit quietly and listen within. Notice the thoughts that continually move through your mind. Allow them to surface without judgment and accept them. Some of the thoughts stir up feelings of anxiety or stress. Concerns about our finances, career, relationships, family issues, and health often get our full attention.

Choose a concern or problem in your life that is unsatisfying. For instance, maybe you feel that the economy, the job market, or more highly qualified job seekers are limiting your career opportunities and success. Perhaps there are problems in your relationship with a family member or you would like to increase your finances and receive more abundance. Contemplate the level of consciousness of your thought or concern.

A thought based in material consciousness gives power to external, tangible forces, what is outside of us. We are victimized by others and things that we cannot control.

Does it appear that what you are experiencing is caused by an outer event or circumstance or that someone else is the cause of the problem or concern you are dealing with?

Does it feel as if the solution to this issue is dependent on another or an external force?

Here are some examples of thoughts and concerns that are based in material consciousness:

- I'm too busy with work and taking care of others to take care of myself. If my family supported my desire to eat better and didn't cause me so much stress, I wouldn't have these health problems.

- I want to make more money and get a better job, but it's hard to get ahead when I don't have the right connections with influential people.

- If my sister wasn't so self-centered and judgmental, we would get along so much better.

- My car broke down and I have bills to pay. Everything seems to be working against me.

Maybe your perception is centered more in mental consciousness. Awareness based in mental consciousness gives power to our thoughts, ideas, and intentions. When we are overly analytical, overthink, and listen to the authoritative voice of the chattering mind, we are enmeshed in mental consciousness.

Thoughts based in mental consciousness go something like this:

- I don't know why my boss didn't give me a promotion. I made a list of everything that I accomplished this year and she still didn't promote me. I did get a bit of a raise, but that's not enough. I need to figure out a better plan and strategy to make things work.

- I can get frustrated with my boyfriend, Jeff. It seems that no matter what I do, he finds something to complain about. Still, there is so much about him that checks all my boxes. He has a good job and is smart and handsome. With enough effort, I should be able to make this relationship work. I think I can help him make some changes.

- I am tired of being broke and having credit card debt. I am going to repeat affirmations to attract more money. If I can just stay positive and say the affirmations over and over again, maybe they will work.

Because mental consciousness is bound to duality, we will always experience both the positive and the negative and what we want and what we don't want. Our ability to fulfill our desires is dependent on our intellect and effort. We might also blame ourselves for not being more positive and creating discouraging or negative circumstances through our thoughts. We may try to make change through affirming the good and coming up with better ideas and strategies.

It is only through spiritual consciousness that we enter into the realm of divine creative activity. When we surrender control, our issues, concerns, and conditions are lifted into a higher frequency of love. Despite how we may see something or how it may appear, spiritual consciousness transforms all things into their highest expression. As we allow the divine force of love to be the activity of our consciousness, our issues and concerns become opportunities for our growth and evolution.

Much of the time, the way we respond to and interpret what we are experiencing is habitual and based in an unconscious pattern. This can change. Once we identify the level of consciousness of our thoughts and emotions, we can more easily shift into a higher awareness.

If you find yourself thinking thoughts or experiencing feelings at a level of consciousness that you would like to shift out of, accept them. Don't push them down or try not to feel what you are experiencing.

Disengage from outer activity and draw your awareness within. Gently guide your thoughts and understanding of what you are experiencing to thoughts of the divine. Remind yourself that there is only one power at work in your life and it always manifests as your highest good. Surrender and let go. Allow divine activity to create something better than what you are expecting or hoping for.

Breathe into your heart and invite the force of love to move through you. Take long, deep, relaxing breaths, exhaling any stress or tension. Continue to breathe and relax until you feel any subtle sensations or feelings of divine presence. This may come to you as a tingle of energy, the release of tension, a heart opening, a sense of inner peace, or feelings of expansion or warmth.

Ask within for the divine interpretation of a specific concern, worry, or problem.

You could ask such things as this:

- What am I learning from this situation or challenge?
- How could this issue be used for my highest good?
- How can I best love myself and express love to others in this situation?
- What is the divine interpretation of this issue or problem?
- How am I blocking the manifestation of abundance?

Listen within and allow whispers of truth, insights, and guidance to stream into your awareness. Ask inwardly for the divine interpretation of your concerns and worries, then make any changes where you can. Rest in the inner quiet, knowing that your good is being worked out.

As you feel and listen within to the subtle whispers, sensations, feelings, and awareness of the divine, accept that you are receiving whatever you need to know at this time. It may arrive in a moment of awareness or insight or more slowly over a period of time.

Over the coming hours, days, weeks, or even months, notice the aha moments when your mind, body, heart, and spirit feel the touch of divine presence and you receive messages and insights of truth. As you recognize higher divine frequency, your sense of self expands, you may feel lighter, or a shiver of energy may move through you. This is the moment when you raise your frequency and the manifestation of your highest good begins to unfold.

Pay attention and watch for any shifts in the conditions and circumstances of your concerns. Be aware of any new perspectives, ideas, flashes of inspiration, or feelings of renewed clarity or inner strength that surface. Act when you feel motivated to or led in a certain direction or when an opportunity surfaces. This may be an increase in financial abundance, new career possibilities, the working out of your concerns and problems with ease, or new relationships with those aligned with your heart and spirit. Remain open and allow whatever is in your highest good to come to you.

Maintaining a High Vibration

When we raise our vibration and frequency, our highest good continually manifests. While it may seem essential to ask and pray for specific things, like physical healing or money to pay our bills or the perfect job, it isn't necessary. When we give power to lack, we lower our vibration into the material realm, and divine activity is no longer at work within our consciousness. When we lift our awareness to a level where there is only infinite supply, this awareness flows into all areas of our lives naturally and without us trying to make it happen.

Keep your awareness focused on the divine creative activity that is always in motion and never falters or ceases. Give way to its desire to create through you and release yourself into your highest good. Release your expectations of how your good will appear and the form of its manifestation. There will be many situations where you won't be able to understand the significance of why things are happening the way they are. The divine is still present. Continue to invite the flow of the force of love to work through you. Even when appearances seem otherwise, trust that the goodness is unfolding.

Our expectations and desires must be worthy of our spirit. If what we desire is not aligned with our heart, soul, and spirit, then the pure joy and love that we long for will not be found. For a time, we might bask in the glow of being wealthy, popular, and successful and having many things. However, the initial high of happiness we experience will eventually dissipate and we will begin to feel the same nagging frustrations and dissatisfaction that we previously felt. The battle with ourselves continues as we again strive to prove our worthiness and ability to conquer and succeed. We go to war with ourselves and life.

When we surrender our ego desires and expectations, we are not giving up control to anything outside of us. Instead, we ascend to the divine within us that is in perfect union and alignment with our highest good. The force of love works from within and is always present and operates in the now. It brings forth abundance where there is lack, healing when there is illness, loving relationships, and perfect joy.

Listen within to the emanations of the divine presence. Let it speak the truth and fill your heart. As we feel and make contact with the force of love, all things come into their natural rhythm. The energy of the divine presence resounding throughout our being is the seed of manifestation.

Moments of Connection

The conscious awareness of the divine presence may occur in a second or a brief moment. It doesn't matter how intense or slight our encounter is. When we experience the highest light within us, limitations evaporate. Small moments of conscious awareness of the divine are powerful and can alter the course of our life. In these moments of communion, we are transformed. The deep beauty of an intimate and expansive love illuminates our being.

However, in the midst of expansive awareness, it isn't unusual for the feelings of love and sense of connectedness to a higher presence to suddenly evaporate. The chattering mind takes over and we find reasons to dismiss or question our experience. The ego creates self-doubt and persuades us to ignore and disregard anything that it cannot control. We may go from feeling the assurance of divine presence to feeling unworthy, being preoccupied with our mistakes, or focusing on other issues entirely. If and when this happens, don't become discouraged, as this is normal. Breathe and simply let go. We don't have to be perfect or flawless to ascend into spiritual consciousness.

The ego attempts to take control by telling us anything to get our attention. We may feel that we need to try harder and struggle to find the good in ourselves. Our ego may try to convince us that contact with the divine is delusional, hopeful thinking, or just our imagination. Doubt and resistance are inherent in material and mental consciousness. We have been programmed to strive and never fully achieve. In the physical world, we will never feel perfect and without issues and problems.

Yet in just a moment of connection with the force of love, the voice of the ego loses its power and we ascend into divine awareness. The more we lift our consciousness into this higher vibration, the more our good manifests in our day-to-day experience. In moments throughout the day and night, consciously connect within the divine. Call out to the force of love to be present and it will respond. Wherever we are and whatever we are doing, a part of us can enter the silence and ask for the divine presence to fill our heart. No matter what is happening around us, we can make the choice to shift our consciousness. It doesn't matter if we are troubled, worried, and stressed or grateful, happy, and at peace; we can always take a moment to breathe and open our mind and heart to the force of love. The more often we consciously connect with the divine, the more power it has in our day-to-day lives.

The skies, the seas, the mountains and valleys, and the beauty and wonder of the earth and all of creation were set in motion by the whisper of the divine. The force of love isn't limited by material laws, and as it flows into our consciousness, neither are we. We, too, receive the rich streams of divine creative activity. Our intuitive and empathic receptivity ushers in the higher vibrations of love, wisdom, guidance, and insights. It is through these quiet whispers that the divine continues its creative activity in the physical world. Our extrasensory abilities become the channel through which all things are possible.

The divine is always present within our heart, soul, and spirit. It is in the inner silence that we make conscious contact with the divine presence and accept the invitation to allow the divine light to enter into our being. The following meditation will help guide you into a more conscious communion with the divine presence.

....

MEDITATION
Conscious Contact with the Divine

Make it a priority to commune with the divine presence on a daily basis. Don't wait for the right time or put it last on your list. Surrendering to and inviting the force of love to be active in our lives is essential. This practice allows the full blessings and bounty of the divine to flow into every aspect of our being.

Create a space in your home to relax and be comfortable, where you will not be disturbed. Inhale relaxing breath and exhale any stress and tension. Imagine the breath moving down through the top of your head. Move the energy of this breath through your body and exhale any tightness, stress, or tension. Continue to breathe in this way.

Exhale and release any of the concerns, worries, or stress that you have been feeling and carrying within your mind and body. If you find yourself getting pulled into emotions as they surface, continue to breathe and fully feel your feelings.

Take as much time as is necessary to come into a relaxed state. Continue to inhale breath down through the top of the head. Move this breath through the body, relaxing and loosening any tension and stress.

When you feel as if you have released and let go of stuffed-down emotions or tension, imagine breathing white-light energy down through the top of your head and through your body. As the white-light breath moves through you, continue to breathe and relax. Feel yourself become lighter and your heart expand. Continue to breathe in this way.

With each breath, exhale through your heart and imagine white-light energy flowing through you and surrounding you. Continue to breathe and fill yourself with this light.

Imagine your awareness expanding and moving beyond the boundaries of your physical body. Feel the lightness of your being as your consciousness expands.

Breathe and feel the force of love flowing through your heart. This love has awareness and wisdom. Listen and feel its presence.

Let go and become aware that there is only one power at work in your life and it desires to express and manifest as your good. There is no opposition to this divine presence as it gently becomes the activity at work within your consciousness. Surrender to this one power and allow it to fill your heart, mind, soul, and body. Listen to its whispers.

Breathe, relax, and open your heart and mind. Become aware of any inner sensations and shifts. Maybe a subtle warmth rises within you. Become aware of tingles of energy, inner calmness, your heart opening and expanding, or a flow of warmth moving through you. As your breathing deepens, perhaps you feel an inner smile, the softness of an inner light, or a gentle inner rumbling.

Instead of feeling calm and open, you may start to overthink and allow the chattering mind to rattle on. Be gentle and allow these thoughts and feelings to pass through you. They have no power.

Continue to breathe and imagine white light flowing through your heart and into every area of your mind, body, and spirit. Listen to, feel, and sense the whispers and insights of this wise and loving presence. There is no power greater than the force of love. Surrender any resistance or hesitation you may have to allowing the force of love to fill your being.

Within what appears to be a problem or challenge or hurt and pain, there is love and goodness. If you are lonely, hurt, feeling hopeless, or in pain or in need, you are not alone. The force of love can never leave you. What is false falls away. Let it go. In this moment, reside within perfect goodness and love.

You are cared for and loved. There is no lack, no suffering, no problem to solve.

Your spirit feels and knows what is in your highest good. Release any expectation of how this will manifest. There is no lack in a universe that is always in a state of unceasing creativity and abundance.

You may want to softly speak this intention:

I open my heart and allow the higher frequency of divine creativity and love to flow through me. I invite divine creative presence to be active in every area of my life. The one power and presence within my consciousness continually manifests as my highest good.

Rest in the presence of love for as long as possible. Then slowly return to normal consciousness when you are ready.

The Shift

Surrender any expectation of how your good will manifest and become aware of how the force of love responds. Where once you may have absorbed the confusing emotions, thoughts, and physical aches and pains of others, the higher vibrations of love now flow through you. As your intuitive and empathic awareness strengthens, you see, know, and feel from a higher perspective. With an open heart and mind, you receive divine whispers, insights, guidance, and inspiring messages that further your highest good and the good of others.

Allow the messages and spontaneous healing from angels, divine guides, and higher beings to be a common occurrence. Through inner knowing, visions, and gentle whispers, be led along your path one step at a time. The events in your highest good will unfold naturally in perfect time. Feel and affirm the inner assurance that your purpose is unfolding and you are being guided.

Along with the infusion of divine messages and strengthened intuitive and empathic ability, the good also shows up in tangible and material ways. Through this communion, you manifest such things as a renewed sense of purpose, opportunities that bring you joy, a fulfilling career, abundance for all of your needs and desires, physical, mental, and emotional healing, and the grace to help, heal, and enlighten others. Continually remind yourself to allow the higher frequency of divine presence to be the activity of your consciousness.

There is a great mystery and wonder within your being that cannot be fully understood. Allow the force of love to flow into your consciousness and transform whatever feels overwhelming, problematic, or unsolvable—if not in this moment, then in the moment after. If not while you are awake, then while you sleep. If not in the way you want, then in a way that is better. Surrender, be humble, and allow the force of love to create through you.

During short breaks throughout your day, even if it's only five minutes, open your mind, heart, and soul to the inner divine presence. Within all of the mundane events and situations that you find yourself in, the force of love is present.

Our spiritual challenge is to remember to continually invite and allow the divine force of love to flow into our consciousness. We do this by listening within to the divine thoughts as they emerge. Focusing on our concerns, worries, and challenges only strengthens their hold on us and further convinces us that we are alone and on our own. Moments of connection and surrendering to the divine are transformative. As the beauty of light unfolds within you, divine presence becomes the activity within your consciousness.

CHAPTER 14

Attunements to Maintain
a Higher Frequency

We are on the precipice of a collective shift into a higher dimension. The influx of higher-frequency energy is moving us out of trying to control and manifest our good through our ego-based sense of self. Instead, we are becoming aware that it is through our communion with divine forces that the gates of manifestation open.

The demands of the world have made us weary. Attaining the things we need for our everyday life has created a culture of anxiousness, fear, and exhaustion. We now know that there is another way. Through surrendering our concerns, worries, and stress and allowing the force of love to flow into our being, our highest good effortlessly manifests. Our needs and desires are met in tangible ways, and we attract the things, opportunities, synchronicities, people, and conditions that are in our highest good.

Make it a daily devotion to invite the force of love to flow into every aspect of your life. Spiritual attunements are a way to heighten the energy frequency of your mind, body, and spirit. To support your ascension into spiritual consciousness, this chapter includes practices, exercises, and meditations on practicing states of being such as joy, innocence, service, compassion, humility, kindness, and forgiveness. These are not just positive thoughts and actions, but portals of energy through which we raise our vibration and allow the force of love to move into every aspect of our lives. Open your heart and mind to the exercises, practices, and meditations within these attunements. As we put divine attributes into action, spiritual consciousness integrates into our everyday life.

As we continually lift our awareness into the higher frequencies, we ascend out of the limitations of the material and mental realms and into the creative freedom of spiritual consciousness.

··

PRACTICE
Collecting Evidence of the Divine Presence

Transitioning from a material and mental consciousness to a spiritual consciousness occurs as we merge with and listen within to the higher frequency of divine presence. While we can have moments of spiritual connection and experiences of manifestation and abundance, doubts and worry can still creep in. To strengthen our awareness and integrate the powerful infusions of spiritual presence into our day-to-day lives, it can be helpful to collect evidence and document in a journal the positive shifts and manifestations of your highest good that occur as you work with the attunements.

Notice the divine presence in the small and often quiet things that occur throughout the day. This may be an assuring inner message or insight, a feeling of love and comfort, or a synchronicity. Perhaps your day unfolds with ease, and worries, stresses, and anxious thoughts subside. You have the heartfelt certainty that everything is going to work out and that you are being guided and watched over. You feel seen, heard, and loved and know that your life has meaning and purpose.

The good may appear in more overt and noticeable ways. For instance, kind, helpful, trustworthy, and loving people come into your life. A new career or financial opportunity arrives with no effort on your part, or you unexpectedly receive a promotion or recognition for a work project. You are inspired by creative ideas and fulfilling ways to be of service to others. You experience mental, emotional, or physical healing or rejuvenation.

Every day, do your best to discover as many occurrences of divine presence at work in your life. Pay attention to any feelings, encounters, expressions of love, or small and simple things or acts that speak to your heart. It doesn't matter if what comes your way is a big or a small expression of divine manifestation. Have gratitude. Expressing a heartfelt thank-you allows the good to multiply. As we acknowledge and express our thankfulness for the greater power that is at work in our lives, we ground, integrate, and increase the flow of spiritual consciousness and manifestation.

Power

Through material and mental consciousness, the world exerts influence and power over our day-to-day lives. The outer world and others seem to influence such things as our moods, what we believe is possible for ourselves, and our sense of safety and power. Our sense of power is often linked to our ability to create the life we desire, how much money we have, and the influence we can exert over others. We may feel powerful when we achieve goals and have success in areas that are important to us and feel inadequate when we think we have failed. Our physical attractiveness, the achievements of our family and friends, and our ability to get what we want also lend us a degree of power.

However, we inevitably go through cycles of feeling both powerful and powerless. When we succeed, we feel a sense of accomplishment. If we don't rise to our expectations, we shrink and feel powerless over our destiny. We might experience angst, depression, and soul exhaustion when we feel we lack personal and worldly power.

For instance, we may stay in relationships, occupations, and abusive situations because we believe we don't have what it takes to create change or make it on our own. Caged within a life that doesn't speak to the authenticity of our heart and soul, we suffer.

While we may succeed through our effort, will, drive, and hard work, our victories may feel hollow. When we are overly concerned with external goals and values that are not aligned with our spirit, we eventually become exhausted and soul-sick.

Through spiritual consciousness, we are introduced to a new understanding of power. Spiritual power is the never-ceasing divine creative activity that elevates everything to its highest potential and expression. When we are aligned with the high vibrations of our spirit, we are in our power.

Unfortunately, we go about our day giving away our power and compromising ourselves in a variety of ways. We all too quickly give up our dreams, highest aspirations, and desires because we believe they are impractical and foolish. We adhere to what the world waves in front of us as power. Such things as money, attractiveness, lucrative career choices, influence over others, and the number of social media contacts we have give us the illusion of power.

For many, it may seem unrealistic and silly to trust that spiritual power is a solution to our everyday physical and material needs. We may believe that there is a separation between spirituality and the *real* world. Spiritual practices can help us reduce stress and anxiety and provide us with a peaceful retreat from our everyday lives. However, we often believe that spiritual power is no match for the demands and struggles of the material world. It doesn't make sense to trust the force of love, which seems distant and removed from the challenges we continually confront. Just contemplating the idea of a spiritual solution to a pressing problem can feel irresponsible and hopeless.

However, when we align with spiritual consciousness, there is no greater power. Worldly and material things are here today and gone tomorrow. True power cannot be taken or given away, lost or diminished. We can lose everything and the force of love will rebuild and re-create it. It is in the whispers of the divine that we are guided and our most potent potential is revealed. When we love ourselves enough to act on our truth despite what others and the outer world dangle in front of us, we harness true power.

To be in your power, say no even if you feel obligated to agree to something that doesn't feel right for you. Listen to your truth instead of the worldly and material voices throughout the day, and act on what you receive. Walk away from opportunities and activities that you know in your heart are not for you. Leave a soul-deadening job and have the courage to pursue the direction of your heart in a more purposeful career. End an abusive relationship instead of telling yourself that your partner will change or that this is the best that it is ever going to get for you. Uncover the unconscious belief that has convinced you that you don't deserve to be treated better. Ask for a promotion or raise or apply for a desired position because you know you are worth it.

Aligning and getting in touch with our power can be a lonely journey at times. When we begin to listen within, we may discover that many of our choices and decisions have been influenced by others and outer forces. We may feel that we have compromised our integrity and allowed cultural conditioning and peer pressure to determine our path. Stepping out of the paradigm of allowing outer influences to dictate our course in life takes courage. Others may disagree and not be happy with our choices. We may find that we no longer have as much in common with friends, coworkers, and family. It can feel like we are stepping off a cliff when we act on the urgings of our heart. However, every small act of listening within and taking back our inner power guides us to our good.

Most of us need to exhaust ourselves, face mounting frustration, or experience loss before we are willing to consider that the happiness that the world promises is an illusion. However, when we surrender and listen within and act on what feels right in our heart and spirit, the force of love comes streaming in. While it can feel as if there are no guarantees that we will succeed or even be okay, it is in the darkest moments when we trust the light within that we activate our true power.

Go within and listen to your heart and spirit. This is where you will discover who you are and your purpose and potential. Call back your power from anyone and anything that you perceive as having more authority than your own heart.

....

EXERCISE
Empowered Choices

Before you make a decision or choice, pause and listen within. When something is right for us, we feel relaxed, inspired, positive, and at ease. Our heart opens and we feel safe. Even if we are nervous about taking a positive step or doing something new or different, the underlying feeling that this is the right choice will be present.

Body tension, stomachaches or headaches, and feelings of stress, fear, and anxiety are indications that something isn't in our highest good.

When you need to make a choice or decision, sit quietly and let go of trying to figure out what to do. Instead, imagine letting go of the issue and releasing it into the higher vibrations of divine activity. Breathe, relax, listen within, and feel the sensations and feelings in your body. Draw your awareness to your solar plexus. This is your place of power.

What choice strengthens, soothes, and calms your heart, stomach, and solar plexus?

What choice creates more stress or fear or a feeling of being disconnected?

Trust what you experience, and even when you don't have any outer verification, act on what brings you a sense of ease, opens your heart, and helps you feel empowered.

....

Being of Service

Being of service is an accelerated path into spiritual consciousness. It doesn't matter what type of service we perform or what we give and share. The demonstration of our love through the activity of service to others and the world is what is essential. Some feel called to contribute financially to worthy causes or share what they can to shelter and feed others, while others use their intuition and healing gifts to tend to the physical, emotional, spiritual, and mental needs of those who are in pain or suffering. There are some who contribute in various ways to the animal and plant worlds or are part of a community that addresses global issues and causes. There are innumerable ways to give, share, heal, and be of service.

Being present to the needs of others or the planet comes naturally for most empaths and the intuitive and sensitive. Unfortunately, we don't always know how to take care of ourselves as we give and open our hearts. Our soul is a magnet that draws us to those who are needy and suffering, and them to us. When we engage with those who are in pain or downtrodden or feel hopeless, we tend to give without restraint. Our boundaries may be loose or nonexistent, and this allows others to take advantage of us or exhaust our energy reserves.

Service work that is divinely inspired opens our heart and motivates us to help and give to others. The higher forces of the heavens are with us when we respond to the immediate needs of another not simply out of guilt or because we think we should or because we want others to think that we are good people. Feeling called to help another as an act of love is a divine calling. A stirring within our heart moves us in a certain direction. Sometimes this takes us by surprise. We may feel a sudden desire to devote ourselves to a particular cause or activity that we hadn't previously thought much about. When we respond to the divine inner urging inviting us to bring hope, assistance, inspiration, courage, and comfort to others, we give in ways that we didn't know we were capable of.

When we respond to the needs of others, angels and divine beings support and amplify our efforts. When I tune into a client's energy during an intuitive session, I quickly know if the person I am reading is selflessly contributing in some way. Angels are present, and not just one or two of them. There may be many light beings supporting and working through us for the betterment of many. The force of love extends its power to those who give, especially when we give without thought of reward. Service work is one of the surest ways to commune with the divine and angels and work in harmony with the heavens.

Through spiritual consciousness, we create a path for divine love, compassion, and goodness to flow into our everyday lives and into the lives of others. Identifying and releasing our repressed emotions and unhealed wounds and disconnecting our energy cords with others allows the light of spiritual consciousness to shine bright in the world. As we become channels of the force of love, high-frequency energy moves through us to others and into the world. Without effort, healing flows through us to those we love, our ancestors, and all others who are ready to receive it. We are not always aware of the influence and effect that embodying higher divine frequencies produces. What emanates from within our heart and soul reaches out beyond the boundaries of the physical realm and into the hearts and consciousness of others.

....
PRACTICE
Evolving through Service

Here are some principles to guide you in being of service to others.

Don't assume you know why things happen to others. We don't know why suffering is so much a part of this world. It is a spiritual mystery. We all experience pain in various ways and to varying degrees. It is a part of the imprint of suffering here on planet earth. However, the love we express through being of service to others helps to shift the planetary paradigm of suffering.

Despite appearances, divine activity is always at work. When you are overwhelmed with the darkness of pain and suffering, allow your suffering to move you beyond the things of the world and into the welcoming warmth and love of your spirit. As you detach and withdraw from materiality, the gentle whispers of the divine inner presence becomes a tangible source of love and comfort.

No matter what form of service you are engaged in, you are always expressing, sharing, and receiving love. Global activism, providing food and shelter to others, caring for the planet and the natural world, healing others, and many other expressions of service are all ways to love.

Although being of service seems to be for the benefit of others, the giver is also rewarded. The path of goodness and well-being cannot be found in money and material things. It comes through the experience of loving and helping others. Service to others opens our heart and provides us with a capacity to receive love that is not possible when we are only concerned about ourselves. Selfless giving is the way of the heavens.

Generously loving through acts of service without any thought of reward and recognition lifts our energy vibration into spiritual consciousness. It grounds and integrates the higher divine frequency into our everyday experience. We evolve and grow in our awareness of self and of spirit.

Gifts that we didn't know we possessed emerge, synchronicities and manifestations of what is needed spontaneously appear, and we have the sure awareness that we are being watched over and protected.

Being of service and giving to others isn't only between you and another; the divine spirit is always present. The call to show up in practical, spiritual, and dynamic ways for others and the world is not driven by what is outside of us, but what is within. When we serve others, we strengthen our connection to the divine.

It is often among those who are the most needy and downtrodden that the force of love can be more fully felt and experienced. Ask within to be led to others, to a cause or goal or activity that is in your highest good and for the good of others.

Beauty

Much of our thought about beauty has been derived from cultural influences and clever advertisers. We have been programmed to believe that beauty lies in such things as a sculpted body and fashionable clothing, cars, and homes. The beauty of physical attractiveness and material things appeals primarily to our senses and not our spirit. While sensual beauty can be enticing and stimulating, we often are left feeling empty and lacking after the initial feelings of elation. External and material beauty may motivate us to compare ourselves and our possessions to others and the current cultural standards. This can lead to self-judgment, where we perceive ourselves as less worthy and feel we are missing out. Beauty that is focused in the material realm fades. It always goes away. We may try to keep up with beauty treatments, lose weight, buy new things, or redecorate, but eventually what we once perceived as beautiful loses its appeal.

Our heart and spirit knows, feels, and perceives another type of beauty. Something wells up within us when we encounter spiritual beauty. We often experience this when in nature. We are awakened to beauty that extends beyond appearances and touches something deep within. Watching the morning sun bring light to the darkness, walking along the endless blue horizon of a seashore, or witnessing a swarm of butterflies gently landing on flower petals stirs our inner senses. Unlike the fleeting feeling of gratification that we may feel when witnessing material beauty, spiritual beauty hints at the beyond.

When we are immersed in the beauty of the natural world, we pause and our worries and stress diminish. This expression of beauty doesn't cause us to overthink or feel less worthy or insecure. Instead, its gentle whisper pulls us into an inner place of quiet and soulful contemplation. In natural beauty, there is peace and comfort. Even a raging river or the wind atop a mountain peak has its own stunning silent beauty. Joy and beauty are intertwined. In the presence of beauty, our heart lifts us into the lightness of being.

Sublime spiritual beauty expressed in physical form is a pure expression and manifestation of the divine. Not only is it pleasing to our physical senses, but it also reminds us that there is something compelling and mysterious present within the ordinary and mundane. True beauty is not expressed exclusively through physicality, but through a divine essence that speaks to our heart.

While we may be able to grasp the divine purpose within such things as love, forgiveness, and kindness, beauty as a spiri tual attribute may seem frivolous and not essential or significant. Yet no matter how much we know, understand, and can dissect about the things of the world, essence is beyond explanation. It draws us closer to the masterful divine creative force and gives us rest from this weary world. Beauty is the haven of the divine. It is the sweet lullaby that comforts us and reminds us that there is a force of love at work in the world and within us. The essence of nature touches something deep within. It nudges, wakes, and reminds us that the divine presence, the creative force, is not judgmental, demanding, distant, or condemning. Instead, the light of the stars on a dark night, the gentle rhythm of the wind through the trees, and the first shoots of spring flowers hint at the existence of a graceful, gentle, and loving divine creative power.

All things that manifest in the physical realm will one day fall away and change, yet the spiritual essence of what was in physical form is indestructible. Despite the ugliness, decay, destruction, pollution, and carelessness we continually witness in the world, the invisible essence of beauty can never be tarnished. It will manifest and be expressed and witnessed again and again in multiple forms. Beauty is an eternal aspect of the divine—a truth that touches our soul and reminds us that we, too, are divine essence and beauty and exist beyond physical form.

Bringing beauty into our everyday experiences promotes spiritual consciousness. Even if we don't live near a majestic mountain range, a babbling brook, or a rocky seashore, we can experience beauty.

PRACTICE
Beauty That Nurtures the Soul

As you go about your day, pause, become aware of your breath, relax, and scan your environment.

Notice such things as a single fresh flower, a painting or photo, the clouds moving across the sky, the smile of another, or the way the sunlight casts shadows.

As you notice the things in your environment, become aware of what you are drawn to. Pause and take this in. Breathe and relax.

Even if what you land on is not particularly beautiful in a conventional way, let it speak to you. Allow the mysterious emergence of soulful appreciation to rise up from within. Beauty is not defined solely by appearance. The spiritual essence of beauty exerts a mysterious influence on our mind and heart and lifts us into the higher frequencies of divine presence.

CHAPTER 15

Kindness

We all have expressed and received kindness from others. When a stranger opens a door or an employee in a busy store takes extra time to help us, it feels good. Kindness is a simple act. It may be a smile, a word of encouragement, listening when we or someone else needs to be heard, or prioritizing another's needs over our own. When we receive kindness from another, it improves our mood and our day is often made better. Even small acts of kindness can be powerful. When we feel seen and cared for, not only does it lighten our mood, but our sense of worthiness improves as well. Our faith in others is renewed and we don't feel so alone in a world that often feels callous and cold.

Being kind to another often has more of an impact than we might realize. Pausing and allowing someone to go first when looking for a parking space or being patient when a parent tries unsuccessfully to quiet their child on an airplane matters, not just because it is helpful to another, but because it is a selfless act. Being kind is not always as easy as it might seem, as it often requires that we become aware of another's needs and wishes and put them before our own.

Sometimes being kind seems to go against the programming that encourages us to be assertive and look out for ourselves. Acts of kindness can diminish our sense of importance and our belief that our primary concern should be to seek our own satisfaction. It goes counter to the self-protective stance of material consciousness that frowns upon giving to another with no thought of return. Acts of kindness are selfless and don't feed our innate instinct to be stronger, better, and more worthy than others. It requires that we have empathy and be aware of others' needs.

Kindness is giving another our gentle and caring full attention, with the desire to lighten their load. We don't do this because it feeds our ego, provides financial gain, or makes us better than others. The impetus to express kindness comes from our wise spirit and loving heart. We are lending our spiritual consciousness and power to another.

The hallmark of being intuitive, empathic, and sensitive is the ability to feel, sense, and be present to others' emotions and energy. However, our ability to sense and feel what others are feeling and experiencing is just the tip of the iceberg. People in need are often pulled into the loving aura of the empath. The desire to love, help, heal, and be there for others is as consistent and ever-present as the beating of our heart. It feels good to give and provides us with a sense of purpose.

Unfortunately, for many empaths, intuitives, and sensitives, being kind can lead to confusion, pain, and regret. Putting others' needs before our own is second nature. However, this makes us easy targets for being taken advantage of, manipulated, and used. Those in need and in pain often sense the deep reservoir of love within empaths. Some knowingly and others unknowingly do all they can to be the recipient of this love.

The depth of soulful love within those who are energy-sensitive can lead to kindness without boundaries. We don't just smile or open the door for another. Instead, we silently respond to others' needs before they are expressed. When someone reveals their wounded heart, we sweep it into our open arms and do our best to make it bright and strong again. Kindness is not a small act for an empath. Instead, it is an energetic exchange where we absorb the energy of others while simultaneously filling them with love. However, we aren't always aware that we are doing this. It is innate and feels natural and good to be able to give … until it doesn't.

Unfortunately the empath's version of being kind can begin to be burdensome, exhausting, and heavy with responsibility. Soaking in the energy of others and responding to their needs often lowers our vibration, and we aren't able to ascend into spiritual consciousness. Instead of being a channel for the divine to enter, we amplify others' troubles, worries, or stress. Over-giving and trying to help another through feeling their feelings and taking on their energy doesn't work. It causes confusion, increases pain, and dulls our connection to the force of love. We might suddenly need to withdraw from others and seek out ways to replenish our inner reserves.

As intuitives, sensitives, and empaths, it is essential that we practice being kind without taking on another's energy. We need to remember to allow the force of love to flow through us to others. Otherwise, we become imbalanced and depleted. When our awareness is focused in the higher vibrations of divine love, we don't absorb the energy of others. Instead, the frequency of love flows outward from our heart and being. As we surrender our judgments of what another needs and allow the divine presence to lead the way, the good manifests.

··

PRACTICE
Kindness That Frees

Small acts of kindness can help us practice giving to others without absorbing toxic or negative energy or allowing ourselves to be taken advantage of.

Every day, commit to an act of kindness, such as allowing another to go first in a line, smiling at and saying hello to strangers, or posting a positive recommendation for an author or a business. Little things such as opening the door for another, giving a genuine compliment, leaving a good tip at a restaurant, or offering to do a favor for another lift us into spiritual consciousness. Invite the divine presence to flow through you to whoever may be in need or is suffering.

Don't look for others to notice or compliment your actions. Simply practice kindness and soak in the positive vibes of how it feels to give generously. Move your awareness into your heart and spirit. If you feel yourself becoming drained or feeling another's burdens and feelings, take a moment to pause, breathe, and become centered. Surrender the energy you are absorbing and your own overwhelmed feelings to the flow of the force of love.

Give often and freely, without expectation.

··

Innocence

We have all felt guilty at one time or another. We may have hurt someone's feelings, been dishonest, acted in a way that went against what we felt was the right thing to do, or been callous to another. We don't always live up to the standards that we set for ourselves and be the kind of person we would like to be. Sometimes feeling guilt can help us grow and evolve out of self-centeredness and focusing only on our own needs. If we hurt another and this doesn't feel good, we are motivated to align our actions with our heart. When feelings of guilt help us recognize that we want to act in accordance with our most loving and wise self, we evolve.

However, there is another type of guilt that empaths, intuitives, and the highly sensitive experience. It is less about what we have done and how we have treated others. Instead, it stems from who we are and the parts of us that we cannot change. This kind of guilt is a form of shame. It is rooted in the unconscious belief that we should be able to be the person that others expect us to be. When we aren't able to act in ways that our parents, friends, partner, and society expect of us, we may feel guilt.

As empaths, intuitives, and sensitives, we aren't always comfortable with such things as shallow conversation and confrontational or loud situations or with people who hide their true motives. This is especially true when we are young and don't fully understand our gifts and who we are.

For instance, others might have enjoyed being in the company of our Uncle Bob and found his jokes funny. However, we sensed something in him that made us want to get away as fast as possible. When he came close to give us a hug, we cringed and became tense.

Maybe we felt, saw, or sensed spirits in our home or someone else's home. If we worked up the courage to say something, we may have been given an odd look, laughed at, or made fun of.

For some, feeling others' emotions, moods, or negativity was confusing. While everyone else may have been acting as if everything was fine, we knew better. Of course, there was always the fear that we were making it up and there was something wrong with us.

We may not have been able to participate in the things that others did and took for granted. We may have been mocked or teased for being overly sensitive and overwhelmed by loud noises and crowds and being overstimulated by too much chaos and activity.

We didn't understand why surprising emotions would suddenly come over us in the company of certain people. We may have avoided certain individuals and later felt guilty for not wanting to be in their company. Not realizing that what we were feeling was the absorbed feelings of another, we might have also felt shame for believing that we were weird or different.

The potency of the emotional energy we absorbed from others or in certain situations and environments might have been so great that we questioned our emotional health. Feeling another's pain, loss, grief, angst, or sadness may have left us feeling confused, depressed, tired, and exhausted.

Maybe we buried our sensitive, intuitive, and empathic nature because we wanted to fit in and be like others. We hid and didn't talk about our feelings and insights and masked our feelings. We might still hide who we are and have residual and unconscious feelings of guilt and shame. The feelings of anxiety and stress, post-traumatic stress disorder, sleep issues, and insecurities we might currently be experiencing could stem from our past. It is not just how others treated us that continues to cause us injury, but also our own self-judgment, guilt, and shame. It's time to surrender this burden.

The cure for shame and guilt is to reclaim our divine innocence. We cannot judge anything or anyone, including ourselves.

Divine innocence is the awareness that we don't know why things happen or the spiritual significance of what we experience.

For instance, perhaps your family and ancestors needed a soul that would usher in a new way of being and break the family mold of inertia and limited patterns.

Without realizing it, you have opened a door for others to evolve and grow. Extrasensory awareness can be the catalyst that energetically alerts others to their own sensitivity and intuitive awareness.

Even though others may have refuted and dismissed your intuitive and empathic nature, they were still energetically influenced by who you are and the energy of your highly evolved heart and spirit.

Any guilt or shame that still lurks within our mind, heart, and being may be preventing us from expressing our true self. This diminishes our power and strength, closes our heart, and keeps us from feeling the joy that is ours to feel. We are here to be who we are and not to suffer the guilt and shame of being sensitive and different. In our heart, we know we have a greater purpose.

Through divine innocence, we perceive and see ourselves and all of life through the lens of wonder. There was a time when everything we experienced was fresh and new. Through curiosity and an open heart, we saw and felt clearly and without judgment. As we grew older, we unconsciously absorbed and accepted others' opinions and cultural and societal norms and expectations. This led to unconscious feelings of guilt or shame. We saw the limited understanding and awareness of those around us as reality. Through spiritual consciousness, we can now perceive ourselves and all of life through the clear lens of divine innocence.

....

MEDITATION
You Are a Gift

If you find yourself worried about what others might think about you, suffer from low self-esteem, or fear that you are powerless in the face of dark and negative influences in the physical or spiritual realms, you may have buried feelings of guilt or shame. Feelings of guilt can show up as trying to be more like others in order to fit in or being embarrassed by your need to create healthy boundaries with others and protect yourself from chaotic and uncomfortable situations. These feelings and others originate in material and mental consciousness and the duality of the world. When we embody our true self, we are free and loving and continually manifest our highest good.

Think of a situation where you denied or hid your true self. Perhaps you needed to take care of yourself with others or were teased for being overly sensitive or strange, and this created feelings of shame or guilt.

Get comfortable and take long, deep, cleansing breaths. Exhale any stress or tension and continue this gentle rhythm of cleansing breath.

Create an image of yourself in a situation where you may have felt guilt or shame for being who you are. See this in as much detail as possible. Stay with this image for a few moments and feel any emotions or feelings that surface.

Imagine that as you inhale, your breath becomes high-vibration white-light energy. Send this energy into your heart and exhale. Allow your breath to connect you to the higher vibrations of love. Feel your heart open, surrounding you with light.

Through the eyes of divine innocence, become aware that there is purpose and meaning in who you are.

Ask within for guidance and greater understanding. Listen within to the whispers of the divine. Allow the light of divine innocence to illuminate your beauty, courage, and love.

Become aware of the gift of intuitive and empathic sensitivity and higher awareness that you embody.

Take your time and listen within. Intuitive insights and understanding may not come immediately. However, your request for guidance and greater understanding will be answered. It could be the next day or a few days later and when you least expect it.

Surrender into the force of love any feelings of guilt or shame that you are aware of and any that you have repressed.

As the force of love moves through you, send this love into the places within you that need love, acceptance, and healing.

As you continue to listen within, rest in the awareness that you are a gift to your family, friends, others, and the planet.

Creativity

During intuitive readings, the topic of creativity sometimes surfaces. Many of my clients will look at me a bit perplexed when I bring this up and tell me that they don't consider themselves creative. They don't paint or do any form of arts and crafts or

design work. Through material understanding, creativity is usually associated with a talent and skill for music, art, design, pot-
tery, and other forms of artistic expression. If we aren't inclined
to participate in an art form or musical talent, we assume that we
are not creative.

It may be difficult to fully grasp the existence of divine creative activity. As the spark of life that never ceases creating
through unlimited potentiality and possibilities, divine creative
activity can never be extinguished. To experience this higher
level of creativity, we must let go and allow for change and transformation. This can feel threatening, as it moves us into the
unknown. We want to live a creative life, but only if we can control it. While we may feel that we are open to possibilities, we
find many reasons to avoid veering away from the familiar.

However, have you ever noticed that even our most thought-
out and organized plans don't always give us the outcome we had
hoped for? Something inevitably comes along, and our plans
go in a different direction or produce an unexpected outcome.
An untamable force or energy may seem to throw our goals and
desires to the wind. Without a sense of control over others, our
situation, or what we want to accomplish, we become stressed
and worried. We may overplan and stick to the predictable out
of fear that if we let things take their natural course, they will fall
apart and bring disappointment or worse.

As we evolve along the path of spiritual consciousness, we
come to the awareness that there is something at work in our
lives that we cannot control. This force is continually moving us
forward into new experiences and opportunities that promote
our growth and evolution. We begin to recognize that change
and transformation are not to be feared. When we embrace this
invisible current, the divine unfurls its creative power within

us. The unceasing and unlimited creative force opens our heart and mind to new ideas, possibilities, and inspiration. When we have the courage to listen to and trust this invisible current, good things happen. We are not bound to the laws of materiality and what may appear to be unattainable and illogical. The higher plan and purpose at work in our lives guides us.

As we move along this evolutionary path, the next step finds us. What is meant for us makes itself known through such things as inspiration, desire, synchronicities, inner knowing, quiet inner whispers, heart-centered awareness, and unexpected encounters. People may come into our life who open us to new ideas or steer us away from futile activities and desires. Sometimes direction comes in the form of obstruction and doors that shut or through the loss and falling away of such things as our job and relationships.

The divine creative force doesn't measure success only through worldly expectations. Many have felt led down a particular path and pursued it with passion but didn't get the results they had hoped for. We may wonder how we could have felt so sure about something only to feel disappointed when it doesn't work out the way we had hoped. However, we are not always able to see and understand why things happen the way they do. What we judge as failure is often the foundation for success. The trust and effort we put into any venture is never wasted. It comes back to us tenfold in other situations and experiences. Often it is only in retrospect that we can see how the puzzle pieces of our experiences fit together.

A creative life is never dull or boring. It is an adventure that allows us to work in tandem with divine creative forces. We can make the magic of creativity an integral part of our everyday life. The universe isn't restrained by limited options. Creativity is the spark that mysteriously brings together the events, circumstances, and people through which a desire, need, or want manifests. While high-vibration divine energy is the core substance through which all things and beings arise, it is creativity that brings them into manifestation.

Here is a simple practice that will help you gain confidence in inviting divine creative activity into your life.

....

EXERCISE
Creative Decision-Making

There is a whimsical aspect to creativity that frees us to reinvent ourselves and get out of our programmed chattering mind. It offers us new perspectives and encourages us to approach life without judgment and preconceived ideas.

You can practice opening to divine creativity in your small daily choices and actions. Before you make a choice or decision, pause, breathe, and relax. Recognize the power of the moment and breathe into your heart and open your mind.

Ponder the choice or decision you are facing. Think of your options and become aware that you might be limiting yourself by what you think is possible. Perhaps there are solutions, ideas, and outcomes that you haven't considered.

Open your mind and heart to possibilities. Be patient, relax, and listen within.

Intuition is one of the channels through which divine creative activity, wisdom, and the playfulness of the universe move into our lives.

As you direct your awareness within and listen, sense and feel what surfaces. Notice when you resist or immediately dismiss an idea or option. Don't reject anything immediately, and give what emerges time to move into your mind and heart.

When we surrender and allow divine creativity to be the activity of our consciousness, what we manifest is so much better than what our limited thinking might produce.

What feels joyful, brings you a sense of peace, opens your heart, and expands your mind? What seems to be calling to you? What feels as if it is opening your heart? What feels right in your gut?

If you are not sure what choice to make, notice any synchronicities, dreams, or desires that surface in the following hours and days.

Once you make a decision or choice, invest yourself fully in it. If you begin to believe that you made the wrong choice, it is okay. When we open ourselves to divine creativity, what is ours will find its way to us. The universe never runs out of clever ways to provide us with our highest good.

Don't judge the outcome as positive or negative, and have gratitude for whatever happens. If you feel confused or unenthused by what occurs, know that in some way your highest good is being nurtured and you are being prepared for greater things.

Humility

Humility is an often overlooked spiritual practice that is essential for our ascension into spiritual consciousness. The programming of material and mental consciousness goes counter to the development of modesty and humility, as it is concerned with harnessing the power of the individual. We are taught to be better, stronger, and more attractive, desirable, and powerful than others. Through both material and mental consciousness, our successes reinforce our sense of self-mastery and importance.

However, beyond the accomplishments and the recognition we receive, stress and the fear of failure lurk. When our self-identity is strongly correlated with our achievements, we must keep applying focus, self-discipline, and effort to maintain feelings of worthiness. There is always someone better, someone more attractive, talented, or clever, nipping away at our accomplishments. We forget that what we create is subject to the law of duality. We can never stay in only the positive or desirable; eventually we will experience the negative and those feelings and events that we would like to avoid. The job promotion, weight loss, new car, or financial increase that we thought would make us happy is only temporarily satisfying. What we create through material and mental consciousness brings us both pleasure and pain.

While we may temporarily feel powerful, success gained through material consciousness is an empty promise. Our power eventually declines, and we often blame ourselves for any loss or disappointment we experience. We tell ourselves that if only we had worked harder and been better, smarter, or more clever, we could have prevented the perceived loss. For many, it is difficult to go without the sense of power that comes with success. Our hunger to be and do better may lead to physical, emotional, and mental exhaustion. The connection of our heart and soul to a greater source of power is muffled background noise.

Humility goes counter to the directives of material and mental consciousness. It is more than downplaying our successes and making our accomplishments seem less important. Through spiritual consciousness, humility is the awareness that it is through our opening to the flow of the divine force of love that we flourish and manifest our good. It is the acknowledgment that what we want, need, and desire doesn't come to us solely through our own efforts. When we raise our vibration into spiritual consciousness, our highest good unfolds.

Humility is a misunderstood and largely ignored expression of spirituality. Natural modesty and humility arise from the awareness of a greater power and presence. Empaths and the intuitive and sensitive have an innate sensitivity that allows us to feel and experience the presence and power of spirit and the unseen. We are often more aware of the divine force of love and can feel how it mysteriously moves through us. Aware that it cannot be manipulated or controlled by human efforts, we listen within for divine whispers and respond to its urgings and guidance.

Being modest and humble releases us from the grip of illusory power and the misguided ego. An inner space is created that the divine force of love fills. We open to the magic of the heavens and trust its direction. Through humility, our personal power moves into alignment with divine presence. Even the mistakes and missteps we make are made right.

Through humility, we have the inner knowing and heartfelt certainty that we are not alone. We are known, loved, and cared for by a greater presence and power. Being humble and modest transports us across the rough waters of the chattering mind and into benevolence and the manifestation of abundance.

Become the billowing sail that is directed and guided by divine winds and led into safe harbor. Be the imperfect being that you are, exactly as you are. You don't have to try to control outcomes or make your good come to you. It is always with you, waiting for you to allow it to move through your being.

....

EXERCISE
The Fullness of Emptiness

Think of a time when you experienced the ease of success or achievement or felt something positive unexpectedly come into your life without stress, worry, or overwork. Feel in your heart and body the delight and gratefulness you experienced.

Take relaxing breaths, exhaling any stress or tension. Imagine that everything that is in your highest good wants to find you and is meant for you. Open your heart and feel the force of love flowing in the direction of your highest good.

Surrender, allow, and feel the sensation of joy and gratitude that comes when you imagine manifesting with ease.

The force of love is more powerful than any limitation or obstacle that you may confront.

When you experience success, abundance, the best outcomes, or unexpected goodness, send a heartfelt thank-you to the higher realms of light. Let the goodness that flows through you extend to others. Humility asks that you share and give to others without seeking outer praise or approval. In this way, the good keeps flowing through you.

....

Joy

Much of our life is spent in pursuit of happiness. We all want to feel good, and there are many things in the material realm that lift our spirits, at least for a time. Exotic trips, lots of money, and new cars, homes, and gadgets make us smile. While there are many things that inspire happiness, we all know that the good feelings are usually temporary. Eventually the delight that we derive through such things fades. Every bright, shiny object that brought us good feelings loses that power. We quickly revert back to the level of happiness that we experienced prior to the uplifting boost.

When our happiness is tied solely to the things of the material world, it is subject to the limitations of duality. This means that our happiness moves along a vast continuum of ups and downs. Positive feelings are fleeting, and soon, frustration, jealousy, dissatisfaction, or boredom comes our way. When happiness takes flight, we try to do all we can to get back to this state. We might buy more things, eat chocolate, find another partner, or fall into the trap of addictions.

Beyond the good feelings that materiality can provide, we also seek happiness through activities and emotional pursuits. Close, loving relationships, a satisfying career, helping others, or traveling and other adventurous activities can elicit laughter and feelings of elation, satisfaction, and positivity. Being able to be in the present moment and engaged in creative activities nurtures happiness.

Joy is a little different. While we may pursue happiness through worldly avenues, joy springs from the heart and soul. It is a transcendent state of being that sneaks up on us when we least expect it. Joy doesn't come to us in the same way as happiness does. Joy is more often unpredictable and a surprise when it occurs. It seems to rumble about in the depths of our soul and emerge in its own time.

Joy is not dependent on what is happening in the outer world. It doesn't come from such things as a job promotion, receiving compliments, acquiring new things, or making a lot of money. The good feelings associated with these kinds of things are more connected to happiness, satisfaction, or pleasure. Joy is a communion with uplifting high-frequency energy. It is divine activity at work within our consciousness that brings forth a lightness that soothes and inspires the heart and soul.

While joy comes from within, we often feel joy with the arrival of an unexpected grace. Has something that you needed or desired ever surprisingly come your way at the perfect time? You may have thought that it was unattainable, and yet, without effort or striving, it showed up. If you have ever received money when you most needed it, a job offer when your options seemed limited, healing when it appeared hopeless, or relief from pain and suffering, you likely know joy. It is not so much the material thing itself that inspires joy. Instead, it is the inner assurance of being cared for and watched over by a loving presence. When we experience a deep sense of comfort in the midst of overwhelming challenges or peace in the midst of loss, we feel joy.

We cannot chase joy or make ourselves feel more joyful. Instead, we have to create the inner environment for it to emerge. Although we aren't always aware of it, joy is always present within our heart and soul. Invite it to rise up from within. Make space for joy by being present to whatever is happening. Resist trying to fix or change something or make it what it is not. Accept things as they are and rest in the awareness that there is only one power at work in your life and it is always directed toward your highest good. In the midst of worries and difficulties, practice compassion and act in loving ways. When we love ourselves and others, we allow joy to emerge.

Whatever outer appearances may suggest, remember that joy springs from our inner activity.

Notice the gentleness of the moment. Kindness and patience toward others and any act of selfless giving open us to joy. When we give of ourselves with no thought of return or expectations, the light of the heavens comes rushing in. Joy rises from our open heart, soft and tender, without cause or reason. It may stay for a moment or bubble up from within randomly throughout the day.

Allow the soft little soldiers of joy in your heart to break through the monotony of mundane life. They bring with them the assurance that there is nothing to do or make happen or acquire to feel good. Joy is your birthright.

....

PRACTICE
Selfless Joy

Joy is the doorway through which the smiles of the heavens well up from within. To create the inner environment for joy to surface, do something in secret for another or a group or for the betterment of the planet. Joy is one of those things that comes to us when we don't focus on it. Pondering a form of selfless giving to another or to a cause may not feel like the path to joy. Instead, it may seem to be a lot of work, and we may feel that we are too busy and don't have the time to add something to our schedule. It's best not to overthink. Try to find a way to give to another that you will enjoy and will be easy. This is one of the paradoxes of spirituality and of joy in particular. Joy doesn't come from doing something that we feel will make us joyful. Instead, it comes when we put someone else's feelings and concerns ahead of our own.

The challenge is to do something for another within a few days of reading this. It is best if this giving is done for someone you don't know and you keep the act to yourself. It must be done from genuine compassion and caring and with an open heart. It may be helpful to think about what stirs up your emotions. This may be in a touching, heartfelt way, or maybe it makes you uncomfortable.

For instance, perhaps when you encounter someone begging for money on the street, you feel uneasy. You may try to ignore a homeless person huddled in a corner on a busy street. Visiting a soup kitchen, helping to build shelter for others, or providing basic necessities to an immigrant may or may not be something you want to do.

Ask within for an opportunity and/or the inspiration to give. Pay attention to what comes your way, or seek out the environment and population you feel called to help. Then do it. If joy doesn't fill your being, keep giving until it does.

Send the message to the joy within that whenever it is ready to surface and spread its warm rays of light and warmth, you will let it have its way.

Forgiveness

It can be hard and seem almost impossible at times to forgive someone who has carelessly or intentionally hurt us. It just doesn't feel right. The three words *I forgive you* don't always whisk away the pain, hurt, and suffering that we experienced. Forgiving another may be one of the most difficult lessons the planet offers us. Pain and suffering at the hands of another can rob us of our innocence, trust, happiness, and sense of well-being. Physical, emotional, mental, and spiritual scars may be carried for a lifetime. Even after a relationship ends or the person who inflicted the pain is no longer in our life, the legacy of suffering can continue.

Suffering is the yoke of this world tied tightly around our neck. Our ego doesn't know how to heal our pain and suffering. It may instead push us to seek revenge and hold onto feelings of anger and bitterness. The chattering mind will repeat over and over the wrongs that we have experienced, intensifying our pain and inciting our anger.

Even though we know that forgiveness may help us let go of the past and move on, it isn't easy. We don't want our suffering to go unacknowledged. Forgiveness can feel like forgetting the injury inflicted on us, which doesn't feel just or right. When we have endured the sting of such things as betrayal, abuse, assault, loss, or manipulation, we don't feel as if we can simply let it go. There seems to be no justice in forgiveness. We want to be made whole and for something of value to be given to us to repair the damage that has been done. Unless we are ready to forgive another, it is not possible to do so. As much as we may try, lingering anger, resentment, pain, and grief may prevent it.

True forgiveness is a powerful spiritual act. To take this step, we have to understand its spiritual significance. Forgiveness is more than a thought, idea, action, or moral obligation. It is a portal that elevates us into a higher-vibration frequency. Spiritually understood, forgiving another for a wrong dulls and disempowers our ego. It brings us to the divine truth that we can never be harmed. What has been hurt and feels damaged is our small self and ego. We suffer to the degree that we believe something can be taken from us and that another's actions are more powerful than our spirit. When we believe that others and the world control our joy, abundance, love, and needs, suffering is inevitable. Being bitter and unable to forgive traps us in a belief system that will always fail us. We have forgotten who we are.

There is nothing another can do to injure our soul. It is impenetrable and doesn't belong to the world or to anyone or anything in the material or mental realm. Always present within us, our spirit is immune to the power and influence of the outer world. Pain and suffering exist in the experience of physicality and our ego. This doesn't mean that our suffering doesn't hurt or isn't important or less significant. However, the power that churns through our being when we forgive another catapults us into spiritual consciousness. We are free. The action taken that caused us pain is no longer ours. It belongs to those who committed the offense. What others do is theirs and always returns to them with equal or greater force. Through spiritual consciousness, whatever injury we suffered and whatever appears to have been taken from us is restored and we are made whole.

Forgiving another doesn't mean that it is safe to be in a relationship with someone who mistreats or abuses you. If we choose to reestablish a relationship with someone we have forgiven, we are vulnerable to being injured again. Unless the offender has an authentic understanding of the pain they initiated and a sincere commitment to change, the pattern will repeat.

Knowing that our soul and spirit cannot be injured allows us to draw strength and healing from within. The inner whispers of divine presence remind us that everything we experience in this world can be beneficial. Paradoxically, being wronged can accelerate our ascension into spiritual consciousness. Being abused, betrayed, or shamed, along with every other type of injury inflicted on us, hurts. The pain is real and it can be long-lasting. However, being wronged gives us the opportunity to forgive, and this is what frees us. Extending grace to another releases us from their grasp and lifts us out of the vibration of material and mental consciousness.

....

EXERCISE
Liberation

You do not have to be in the physical presence of the person you want to forgive to do this exercise. True forgiveness occurs within our own heart, mind, and soul.

Before we can forgive another, we have to allow our emotions to surface without judgment. It isn't possible to move forward until we feel our anger, sadness, disappointment, rejection, betrayal, and any other emotion.

If you want to free yourself and forgive another, begin by inviting your feelings to surface. Give yourself plenty of time and space to allow whatever has been denied or suppressed to become known. We are accustomed to repressing, avoiding, and minimizing hurtful and uncomfortable feelings and don't always recognize the degree of our pain.

Once you have felt and released the emotions surrounding the person you are ready to forgive, create an image of them. See them in your mind's eye in as much detail as possible. If you aren't comfortable visualizing the person, you can simply say their name. Send this person a thought and feeling message expressing all that you would like to say to them. You may want to convey your anger and pain and share the degree to which they hurt you. If you have little or nothing to express, that is fine too.

See this person in their true powerlessness. They cannot hurt you, and you are safe.

When you are ready, say, "I forgive you, (person's name)." This can be done aloud or through your thoughts. If you say the words but don't feel that you are able to truly forgive the person, that is okay. Take some time to continue to feel your emotions, and try again when you feel more ready.

Breathe in the freedom that comes when you let yourself, another, and the world know that the other person's energy does not own you. You are free and whole. Release the burden of carrying their energy. Give back to them the responsibility for their actions and thoughts and the pain they caused you. Send them the thought message that you will no longer share in the energy suffering with them. Whatever pain they have set in motion through their actions and words belongs to them. As you forgive, you release this pain back to them with the awareness that through the divine presence, they too will heal.

You can choose to have this person in your life or not. Forgiveness doesn't mean that you will continue to have a relationship or that you will forget the past. Every situation is different. Trust yourself and always ask within for what is in your highest good.

When you forgive another, they feel it. They may reach out to you and want to reestablish the unhealthy connection you shared. Be careful and listen to your intuition.

Observe their actions and not just their words to know if you can trust them.

When we forgive another, we are lifted into the higher vibrations of spiritual consciousness where love and goodness flow freely. What has been taken from us is restored, and the emptiness that the pain has carved out within us fills with holy light.

Love

The world is in need of light, the kind of light that dispels darkness and opens us to a new way. We need hope and a channel through which our highest aspirations can be actualized and fully lived. Every day we are confronted with the material world and its challenges. Many people struggle with lack, depression, ill health, anxiety, and loneliness. With our thoughts and emotions enmeshed in material consciousness, our intuitive radar often scans our environment for anyone or anything that may contribute to our fear and uncertainty. Our intuitive and empathic sensitivity has adopted a stress response to the situations and circumstances that we confront daily. We have created a view of the world that is fueled by worry, anxiety, insecurity, and false threats. These threats feel and look real, and in our fear we give our power over to them.

However, we are undergoing a planetary awakening as higher frequencies of energy are becoming more available. When we clear our physical and energy bodies of stuck emotions and release unhealthy energy cords, we don't attract difficult and fear-based experiences. We are free from the past and the repeating cycles of negativity and toxic emotions. Divine presence becomes the activity of our consciousness. It is no longer necessary for us to learn lessons and evolve through pain and suffering. The worldly paradigm of struggle and the belief that it is through our individual efforts alone that we thrive is shifting. Instead, as we work in unison with divine presence and surrender to and allow the force of love to move through us, our highest good unfolds.

This shift into spiritual consciousness begins with opening our heart and loving. When we love without judgment, expectation, or need, our love is pure. It doesn't matter so much what we love, but that we love. Loving ourselves, others, and the stuff of everyday life allows and invites the powerful current of the force of love to flow though us.

Love something until you are able to love everything. See the beauty and grace in small things such as a cup of hot coffee on a cold morning, the feeling that a loved one on the other side is with you, and the working out of a problem or concern with ease. Love your pets, the sunrise, the clouds drifting across the sky, a piece of art, and the softness of your pillow. Find something to love in everyone. Even if it is someone you don't get along with, find something about them to love. It may be something as simple as their hairstyle, the effort they put into their work, their dedication to their family, or their laugh. Above all else, love yourself.

When we find something to love in everyone and everything we encounter, the higher current of the force of love flows through us. While we may feel and intuit the emotions, thoughts, and energies of others and our surroundings, they pass through us. Although we may still empathically sense and feel the unhealed wounds and repressed energies of others, we don't react to them from a place of fear and resistance. We don't absorb negative and toxic energy, and our heart doesn't close or shut down. We feel and sense the love that resides within others, even if they don't. However, we are not naive. We know that unless someone chooses to heal, their wounds will leak into every aspect of their life in some way. We don't pity them for this. This is a stage of development that we all must pass through, and we can send others love and let them go at their own pace. Our intuitive and empathic sensitivity becomes the channel through which gentle, divine whispers guide us and the wonder of creative abundance unfolds.

Through spiritual consciousness, we recognize that everything and everyone has value and is either asking for love or expressing love. Oftentimes it is both. There is something we can give to others and something they can offer us. When we love freely, without the thought of return, the divine force of love moves through us. While it may seem to be an ineffectual way to confront our challenges and problems and the ills and suffering in the world, it is through love that we ascend into spiritual consciousness. We become a beacon through which the force of love ignites the love within others. Love is the substance through which all of life and all beings are nurtured and sustained. It is the little drop of divine magic that conceives of and births all that is and all that is to come.

As you awaken to your destiny as a messenger of the higher divine frequencies of the force of love, let go and allow. When you step out of the material paradigm of needing to control and make your good happen, you lead the way for others. In the past, your empathic and intuitive sensitivity allowed the negativity of the world and the down moods of others to adversely influence and affect you. Through spiritual consciousness, you become the channel through which the divine spreads its wings and touches the hearts and minds of many. Your ascension into spiritual consciousness illuminates the darkness as the light of divine presence enters the world. All of this happens naturally and without effort.

The current of divine creative activity flows unceasingly in the direction of your highest good and is a source of goodness for all. Allow yourself the spiritual gift of the joy, abundance, and ease that comes with your conscious connection to the divine source.

Recommended Reading

Afua, Queen. *Sacred Woman: A Guide to Healing the Feminine Body, Mind, and Spirit*. Random House, 2001.

Cameron, Julia. *Waking in This World: The Practical Art of Creativity*. Penguin Books, 2003.

Cayce, Edgar. *The Power of Your Mind*. A.R.E. Press, 2010.

Franken, Kris. *Wildhearted Purpose: Embrace Your Unique Calling & the Unmapped Path of Authenticity*. Llewellyn, 2023.

Goldsmith, Joel S. *The Art of Spiritual Healing*. Acropolis Books, 2018.

Orloff, Judith. *The Empath's Survival Guide: Life Strategies for Sensitive People*. Sounds True, 2018.

Seth. *Seth Speaks: The Eternal Validity of the Soul*. Channeled by Jane Roberts. New World Library, 1994.

Todeschi, Kevin J. *Edgar Cayce's Twelve Lessons in Personal Spirituality*. Yazdan, 2010.

Tolle, Eckhart. *A New Earth: Awakening to Your Life's Purpose*. 2005. Reprint, Penguin, 2008.

Tubali, Shai. *Llewellyn's Complete Book of Meditation: A Comprehensive Guide to Effective Techniques for Calming Your Mind and Spirit.* Llewellyn, 2023.

Tzu, Lao. *Tao Te Ching.* Translated by Sam Torode and Dwight Goddard. Independently published, 2019.

Yogananda, Paramahansa. *Autobiography of a Yogi.* 1946. Reprint, Crystal Clarity Publishers, 2005.

Bibliography

Goldsmith, Joel S. *The Thunder of Silence*. Acropolis Books, 2018.

Hicks, Esther, and Jerry Hicks. *The Vortex: Where the Law of Attraction Assembles All Cooperative Relationships*. Hay House, 2019.

Julian, of Norwich. *All Will Be Well: 30 Days with Julian of Norwich*. Compiled by Richard Chilson. Ave Maria Press, 2008.

Schucman, Helen, and William Thetford. *A Course in Miracles*. Course in Miracles Society, 2009.

To Write to the Author

If you wish to contact the author or would like more information about this book, please write to the author in care of Llewellyn Worldwide Ltd. and we will forward your request. Both the author and the publisher appreciate hearing from you and learning of your enjoyment of this book and how it has helped you. Llewellyn Worldwide Ltd. cannot guarantee that every letter written to the author can be answered, but all will be forwarded. Please write to:

Sherrie Dillard
℅ Llewellyn Worldwide
2143 Wooddale Drive
Woodbury, MN 55125-2989

Please enclose a self-addressed stamped envelope for reply,
or $1.00 to cover costs. If outside the U.S.A., enclose
an international postal reply coupon.

Many of Llewellyn's authors have websites with additional information and resources. For more information, please visit our website at http://www.llewellyn.com.